Joseph Earle Stevens

Yesterdays in the Philippines

Joseph Earle Stevens

Yesterdays in the Philippines

ISBN/EAN: 9783743323391

Manufactured in Europe, USA, Canada, Australia, Japa

Cover: Foto ©ninafisch / pixelio.de

Manufactured and distributed by brebook publishing software (www.brebook.com)

Joseph Earle Stevens

Yesterdays in the Philippines

YESTERDAYS IN THE PHILIPPINES

BY

JOSEPH EARLE STEVENS

AN EX-RESIDENT OF MANILA

ILLUSTRATED

NEW YORK
CHARLES SCRIBNER'S SONS
1899

CONTENTS

INTRODUCTION . . . . *Page xiii*

I

Leaving " God's Country "—Hong Kong—Crossing to Luzon—Manila Bay—First View of the City—Earthquake Precautions—Balconies and Window-gratings—The River Pasig—Promenade of the Malecon—The Old City—The Puente de España—Population—A Philippine Bed—The English Club—The Luneta—A Christmas Dinner at the Club, ... *Page 1*

II

Shopping at the " Botica Inglesa "—The Chit System—Celebrating New Year's Eve—Manila Cooking Arrangements—Floors and Windows—Peculiarities of the Tram-car Service—Roosters Everywhere—Italian Opera—Philippine Music—The Mercury at 74° and an Epidemic of " Grippe "—Fight Between a Bull and a Tiger —A Sorry Fiasco—Carnival Sunday, ... *Page 22*

III

A Philippine Valet—The Three Days Chinese New Year—Marionettes and Minstrels at Manila—Yankee Skippers—Furnishing a Bungalow—Rats, Lizards, and Mosquitoes—A New Arrival—Pony-races in Santa Mesa—Cigars and Cheroots—Servants —Cool Mountain Breezes—House-snakes—Cost of Living—Holy Week, ... *Page 43*

IV

An Up-country Excursion—Steaming up the River to the Lake—Legend of the Chinaman and the Crocodile—Santa Cruz and Pagsanjan—Dress of the Women—Mountain Gorges and River Rapids—Church Processions—Cocoanut Rafts—A "Carromata" Ride to Paquil—An Earthquake Lasting Forty-five Seconds—Small-pox and other Diseases in the Philippines—The Manila Fire Department—How Thatch Dealers Boom the Market—Cost of Living, ... *Page 60*

V

Visit of the Sagamore—Another Mountain Excursion—The Caves of Montalvan—A Hundred-mile View—A Village School—A "Fiesta" at Obando—The Manila Fire-tree—A Move to the Seashore—A Waterspout—Captain Tayler's Dilemma—A Trip Southward—The Lake of Taal and its Volcano—Seven Hours of Poling—A Night's Sleep in a Hen-coop, ... *Page 87*

VI

First Storm of the Rainy Season—Fourth of July—Chinese "Chow" Dogs—Crullers and Pie and a Chinese Cook—A Red-letter Day—The China-Japan War—Manila Newspapers—General Blanco and the Archbishop—An American Fire-engine and its Lively Trial—The Coming of the Typhoon—Violence of the Wind—The Floods Next—Manila Monotony, ... *Page 112*

VII

A Series of Typhoons—A Chinese Feast-day—A Bank-holiday Excursion—Lost in the Mist—Los Baños—The "Enchanted Lake"—Six Dollars for a Human Life—A Religious Procession—Celebration of the Expulsion of the Chinese—Bicycle Races and Fireworks, ... *Page 137*

CONTENTS

VIII

A Trip to the South—Contents of the "Puchero"—Romblon—Cebu, the Southern Hemp-centre—Places Touched At—A Rich Indian at Camiguin—Tall Trees—Primitive Hemp-cleaners—A New Volcano — Mindanao Island — Moro Trophies—Iligan—Iloilo—Back Again at Manila, ... *Page 149*

IX

Club-house Chaff—Christmas Customs and Ceremonies—New Year's Calls—A Dance at the English Club—The Royal Exposition of the Philippines—Fireworks on the King's Fête Day—Electric Lights and the Natives—The Manila Observatory—A Hospitable Governor—The Convent at Antipolo, ... *Page 173*

X

Exacting Harbor Regulations—The Eleanor takes French Leave—Loss of the Gravina—Something about the Native Ladies—Ways of Native Servants—A Sculptor who was a Dentist—Across the Bay to Orani—Children in Plenty—A Public Execution by the Garrote, ... *Page 195*

XI

Lottery Chances and Mischances—An American Cigarette-making Machine and its Fate—Closing up Business—How the Foreigner Feels Toward Life in Manila—Why the English and Germans Return—Restlessness among the Natives—Their Persecution—Departure and Farewell, ... *Page 213*

CONCLUSION . . . . *Page 230*

LIST OF ILLUSTRATIONS

	Facing page
How We Dressed for $2.50	*Frontispiece*
Our Office and the Punkah under which the Old Salts Sat for Free Sea Breezes	8
Plaza de Cervantes, Foreign Business Quarter	14
Puente de España. Manila's Main Highway Across the Pasig	20
The Busy Pasig, from the Puente de España	26
A Philippine Sleeping-machine	32
The English Club on the Banks of the Pasig	40
The Bull and Tiger Fight—Opening Exercises	46
Suburb of Santa Mesa	54
Our Destination was a Town Called Pagsanjan at the Foot of a Range of Mountains	60
The Rapids in the Gorges of Pagsanjan	66
Cocoanut Rafts on the Pasig, Drifting down to Manila	72
The Little Native School under the Big Mango-tree	78
Calzada de San Miguel	84
A Native Village Up Country	90
A "Chow" Shop on a Street Corner	98
Puentes de Ayala, which Help two of Manila's Suburbs to Shake Hands Across the Pasig	106
Calzada de San Sebastian	114

LIST OF ILLUSTRATIONS

Facing page

Ploughing in the Rice-fields with the Carabao	122
Types of True Filipinos Waiting to Call Themselves Americans.	130
On the Banks of the Enchanted Lake	138
In the Narrow Streets of Old Manila. A Procession	144
A Citizen from the Interior	152
How the World's Supply of Manila Hemp is Cleaned	160
Moro Chiefs from Mindanao	168
Manila Fruit-girls in a Street-Corner Attitude	176
A Typical "Nipa" House	184
The Little Flower-girl at the Opera	192
Rapid Transit in the Suburbs of Manila	202
The Fourth of July, '95. Execution by the Garrote	210
Paseo de la Luneta	220
Captain Tayler, the Genial Skipper of the Esmeralda	226
Map of Philippines	*At End of Volume*

INTRODUCTION

By the victory of our fleet at Manila Bay, one more of the world's side-tracked capitals has been pulled from obscurity into main lines of prominence and the average citizen is no longer left, as in days gone by, to suppose that Manila is spelt with two l's and is floating around in the South Sea somewhere between Fiji and Patagonia. The Philippines have been discovered, and the daily journals with their cheap maps have at last located Spain's Havana in the Far East. It is indeed curious that a city of a third of a million people—capital of a group of islands as large as New England, New York, Delaware, Maryland, and New Jersey, which have long furnished the whole world with its entire supply of Manila hemp, which have exported some 160,000 tons of sugar in a single year and which to-day produce as excellent tobacco as that coming from the West Indies—it is curious, I say, that a city of this size should have gone so long unnoticed and misspelt. But such has been the case, and until Admiral Dewey fired the shots that made Manila heard round the world, the people of these United States—with but few exceptions—lived and died without knowing where the stuff in their clothes-lines came from.

Now that the Philippines are ours, do we want them? Can we run them? Are they the long-looked-for El Dorado which those who have never been there suppose? To all of which questions—even at the risk of being called unpatriotic—I am inclined to answer, No.

Do we want them? Do we want a group of 1,400 islands, nearly 8,000 miles from our Western shores, sweltering in the tropics, swept with typhoons and shaken with earthquakes? Do we want to undertake the responsibility of protecting those islands from the powers in Europe or the East, and of standing sponsor for the nearly 8,000,000 native inhabitants that speak a score of different tongues and live on anything from rice to stewed grasshoppers? Do we want the task of civilizing this race, of opening up the jungle, of setting up officials in frontier, out-of-the-way towns who won't have been there a month before they will wish to return?

Do we want them? No. Why? Because we have got enough to look after at home. Because—unlike the Englishman or the German who, early realizing that his country is too small to support him, grows up with the feeling that he must relieve the burden by going to the uttermost parts of the sea—our young men have room enough at home in which to exert their best energies without going eight or eleven thousand miles across land and water to tropic islands in the Far East.

Can we run them? The Philippines are hard material with which to make our first colonial experiment, and seem to demand a different sort of treatment from that which our national policy favors or has had experience in giving. Besides the peaceable natives occupying the accessible towns, the interiors of many of the islands are filled with aboriginal savages who have never even recognized the rule of Spain—who have never even heard of Spain, and who still think they are possessors of the soil. Even on the coast itself are tribes of savages who are almost as ignorant as their brethren in the interior, and only thirty miles from Manila are races of dwarfs that go without clothes, wear knee-bracelets of horsehair, and respect nothing save the jungle in which they live. To the north are the Igorrotes, to the south the Moros, and in between, scores of wild tribes that are ready to dispute possession. And is the United States prepared to maintain the forces and carry on the military operations in the fever-stricken jungles necessary in the march of progress to exterminate or civilize such races? Have we, like England for instance, the class of troops who could undertake that sort of work, and do we feel called upon to do it, when the same expenditure at home would go so much further? The Philippines must be run under a despotic though kindly form of government, supported by arms and armor-clads, and to deal with the perplexing questions and perplexing difficulties that arise, needs knowledge gained by experience, by having dealt with other such problems before.

Are the Philippines an El Dorado? Like Borneo, like Java and the Spice Islands, the Philippines are rich in natural resources, but their capacity to yield more than the ordinary remuneration to labor I much question. Leaving aside the question of gold and coal, in the working of which, so far, more money has been put into the ground than has ever been taken out, the great crops in these islands are sugar, hemp, and tobacco. The sugar crop, to be sure, has the possibilities that it has anywhere, where the soil is rich and conditions favorable. The tobacco industry has perhaps more possibilities, and might be made a close rival to that in Cuba. But the hemp crop is limited by the world's needs, and as those needs are just so much each year, there is no object in increasing a supply which up to date has been adequate. There are foreigners in the Philippines, who have been there for years, who have controlled the exports of sugar or hemp or tobacco, who have made their living, and who from having been longer on the ground should be the first to improve the opportunities that may come with the downfall of Spanish rule. There are some things which the United States can send to the Philippines cheaper than the Continental manufacturers, but not many. She can send flour and some kinds of machinery, she can put in electric plants, she can build railways, but at present she can't produce the cheap implements, and the necessaries required by the great bulk of poor natives at the low price which England and Germany can.

The Philippines are not an El Dorado simply because for the first time they have been brought to our notice. They should not yield more than the ordinary return to labor, and the question is, does the average American want to live in a distant land, cut off from friends and a civilized climate, only to get the ordinary return for his efforts? To which, even though of course there is much to be said on the other side, I would answer, No. We have gone to war, remembering the Maine, to free Cuba, and at the first blow have taken another group of islands—a Cuba in the East—to deal with. I have not the space here to discuss the solution of the problem, but, for my part, I should like to see England interested in buying back an archipelago which she formerly held for ransom, leaving us perhaps a coaling port, and opening up the country to such as chose to go there. Then, with someone else to shoulder the burden of government and protection, we should still have all the opportunities for proving whether or not the islands were the El Dorado dreamed of in our clubs or counting-rooms.

At the close of 1893, I went to Manila for Messrs. Henry W. Peabody & Co., of Boston and New York, in the interest of their hemp business, and, associated with Mr. A. H. Rand, remained there for two years. We two were the representatives of the only American house doing business in the Philippines, and made up practically fifty per cent. of the American business colony in Manila. The years from 1894 to 1896 were peculiarly peaceful with the quiet coming before the storm, and we were fortunate enough to be able to make many excursions and go into many parts of the island that later would have been dangerous. But as the short term of our service drew to a close, rumors of trouble began to circulate. The natives had long suffered from the demands made by the Church and the tax-gatherer, and there was a feeling that they might again attempt to throw off the Spanish yoke, as they attempted, without success, some years before. It was at this period that Messrs. Peabody & Co. decided it would be to their unquestionable advantage to retire from the islands and to place their business in the hands of an English firm, long established on the ground, and well equipped with men who, unlike ourselves, looked forward to passing the rest of their days in the Philippines. And the move was a good one, for no sooner had we left Manila than revolution broke out. The Spanish troops were at the south, and that mysterious native brotherhood of the Katipunan called its members to attack the capital. A massacre was planned, but the right leaders were lacking and the attempt failed. The troops were recalled, guards doubled, drawbridges into old Manila pulled up nightly, arrests and executions made. As is well known, one hundred suspects were crowded into that old dungeon on the river, just at the corner of the city wall, and because it came on to rain at night-fall, an officer shut down the trap-door leading to the prisoners' cells to keep out the water. But it also kept out the air, and next morning sixty out of the one hundred persons were suffocated. Then Manila had her Black Hole. Later, other suspects were stood on the curbing that surrounds the Luneta and were shot down while the big artillery band discoursed patriotic music to the crowds that thronged the promenade. And from then until Admiral Dewey silenced the guns at Cavité and sunk the Spanish ships that used to swing peacefully at anchor off the breakwater, the Spaniards had their hands full with a revolution brought on by their own rotten system of government.

If in place of the more systematic narratives of description, the more serious presentations of statistics, or the more exciting accounts of the bloody months of the revolution and the wonderful victory of our gallant fleet, which are to be looked for from other sources, the reader cares to get some idea of casual life in Manila, by accepting the rather colloquial chronicle of an ex-resident that follows, I shall have made some little return to islands that robbed me of little else than two years of a more hurried existence in State Street or Broadway.

YESTERDAYS IN THE PHILIPPINES

I

Leaving "God's Country"—Hong Kong—Crossing to Luzon—Manila Bay—First View of the City—Earthquake Precautions—Balconies and Window-Gratings—The River Pasig—Promenade of the Malecon—The Old City—The Puente de España—Population—A Philippine Bed—The English Club—The Luneta—A Christmas Dinner at the Club.

"I wouldn't give much for your chances of coming back unboxed," said the Captain to me, as the China steamed out from the Golden Gate on the twenty-five day voyage to Hong Kong via Honolulu and Yokohama.

"That's God's country we're leaving behind, sure enough," said he, "and you'll find it out after a week or two in the Philippines. There's Howe came back with us last trip from there; almost shuffled off on the way. Spent half a year in Manila with smallpox, fever, snakes, typhoons, and earthquakes, and had to be carried aboard ship at Hong Kong and off at 'Frisco. Guess he's about done for all right."

And as Howe happened to be the unfortunate

whose place in Manila I was going to take, you know,
I heeded the skipper's advice and looked with more
fervor on God's country than I had for some days.
For it was a dusty trip across country from Boston
on the Pacific express; and because babies are my pet
aversion every mother's son of them aboard the train
was quartered in my car—three families moving West
to grow up with the country, and all of them occupying the three sections nearest mine. I got so weary
of the five cooing, coughing, crying "clouds-of-glory-
trailers," that it seemed a relief at San Francisco to
wash off the dust of the Middle West and get aboard
the P. M. S. Company's steamer China bound for the
far East.

But the Captain, like the whistle, was somewhat of
a blower, and liked to make me and the missionaries
aboard feel we were leaving behind all that was de-
sirable. And how he bothered the twoscore or
more of them bound for the up-river ports of Middle
China! When, after leaving the Sandwich Islands,
the voyage had proceeded far enough for everybody
on the passenger-list to get fairly well acquainted
with his neighbors, these spreaders of the gospel followed the custom established by their predecessors
and made plans for a Sunday missionary service.
Without so much as asking leave of the skipper, they
posted in the companion-way the following notice:

> Service in the Saloon,
>
> Sunday, 10 A.M.
>
> Rev. X. Y. Z. Smith, of Wang-kiang, China, will speak on mission work on the Upper Yangtse.
> All are invited.

But they counted without their host. The Captain had never schooled himself to look on missionaries with favor, and he accordingly made arrangements to cross the meridian where the circle of time changes and a day is dropped early on Sunday morning. He calculated to a nicety, and as the passengers came down to Sabbath breakfast they saw posted below the other notice, in big letters, the significant words:

> **Sunday, Nov. 29th.**
> **Ship crosses 180th meridian**
> **9.30 A.M.,**
> **After which it will be Monday.**

In Yokohama and Hong Kong the wiseacres were free in saying they wouldn't be found dead in Manila or the Philippines for anything. They had never been there, but knew all about it, and seemed ready to wave any one bound thither a sort of never'll-see-you-again farewell that was most affecting. It is these very people that have made Manila the side-tracked capital that it is and have scared off globe-trotters from making it a visit on their way to the Straits of Malacca and India.

Hong Kong, the end of the China's outward run, bursts into view after a narrow gateway, between inhospitable cliffs, lets the steamer into a great bay which is the centre of admiration for bleak mountain-ranges. The city, with its epidemic of arcaded balconies, lies along the water to the left and goes stepping up the steep slopes to the peak behind, on whose summit the signal-flags announce our arrival. The China has scarcely a chance to come to anchor in peace before a storm of sampans bite her sides like mosquitoes, and hundreds of Chinawomen come hustling up to secure your trade, while their lazy husbands stay below and smoke.

Hong Kong rather feels as if it were the "central exchange" for the Far East, and from the looks of things I judge it is. The great bay is full of deep-water ships, the quays teem with life, and the streets are full of quiet bustle. It is quite enough to give one heart disease to shin up the hills to the residence part of the town, and it took me some time to find breath enough to tell the Spanish Consul I wanted him to visé my passport to Manila.

This interesting stronghold of Old England in the East is fertile in descriptive matter by the wholesale, but I can't rob my friends in the Philippines of more space than enough to chronicle the doings of a Chinese tailor who made me up my first suit of thin tweeds. Ripping off the broad margin to the Hong Kong *Daily Press*, he stood me on a box, took my measure with his strip of paper, making sundry little tears along its length, according as it represented length of sleeve or breadth of chest, and sent me off with a placid "Me makee allee same plopper tree day; no fittee no takee." And I'm bound to say that the thin suits Tak Cheong built for $6 apiece, from nothing but the piece of paper full of tears, fit to far greater perfection than the system of measurement would seem to have warranted.

The voyage from Hong Kong to Manila, 700 miles to the southeast, is one of the worst short ocean-crossings in existence, and the Esmeralda, Captain Tayler, as she went aslant the seas rolling down from Japan, in front of the northeast monsoon, developed such a corkscrew motion that I fear it will take a return trip against the other monsoon to untwist the feelings of her passengers. On the morning of the second day, however, the yawing ceased; the skipper said we were under the lee of Luzon, the largest and most northern island of the Philippines, and not long after the high mountains of the shore-range loomed up off the port bow. From then on our chunky craft of 1,000 tons steamed closer to the coast and turned headland after headland as she poked south through schools of flying-fish and porpoises.

By afternoon the light-house on Corregidor appeared, and with a big sweep to the left the Esmeralda entered the Boca Chica, or narrow mouth to Manila Bay. On the left, the coast mountains sloped steeply up for some 5,000 feet, while on the right the island of Corregidor, with its more moderate altitude, stood planted in the twelve-mile opening to worry the tides that swept in and out from the China Sea. Beyond lay the Boca Grande, or wide mouth used by ships coming from the south or going thither, and still beyond again rose the lower mountains of the south coast. In front the Bay opened with a grand sweep right and left, till the shore was lost in waves of warm air, and only the dim blue of distant mountains showed where the opposite perimeter of the great circle might be located.

It was twenty-seven miles across the bay, and the sun had set with a wealth of color in the opening behind us before we came to anchor amid a fleet of ships and steamers off a low-lying shore that showed many lights in long rows. Next morning Manila lay visibly before us, but failed to convey much idea of its size, from the fact that it stretched far back on the low land, thus permitting the eye to see only the front line of buildings and a few taller and more distant church-steeples. Not far in the background rose a high range of velvet-like looking mountains whose tops aspired to show themselves above the clouds, and on the right and left stretched flanking ranges of lower altitude.

In due season my colleague came off to the anchorage in a small launch, and we were soon steaming back up a narrow river thickly fringed with small ships, steamers, houses, quays, and people. It was piping hot at the low custom-house on the quay. Panting *carabao*—the oxen of the East—tried to find shade under a parcel of bamboos, shaggy goats nosed about for stray bits of crude sugar dropped from bags being discharged by coolies, piles of machinery were lying around promiscuously dumped into the deep mud of the outyards, natives with bared backs gleaming in the sun were lugging hemp or prying open boxes, and under-officials with sharp rods were probing flour-sacks in the search for contraband. Spanish officials in full uniform, smoking cigarettes, playing chess, and fanning themselves in their comfortable seats in bent-wood rocking-chairs, were interrupted by our arrival, and made one boil within as they upset the baggage and searched for smuggled dollars.

Here, then, was the anti-climax to the long journey of forty days from Boston, and those were the moments in which to realize the meaning of the expression made by the Captain of the China as she left the Golden Gate: "Take a last look, for you're leaving behind God's country."

Before arrival, while yet the Esmeralda was steaming down the coast, I was resolved to refrain from judging Manila by first impressions. I felt primed for anything, and was bound to be neither surprised nor disappointed. At first, I may admit, my chin and collar drooped, but on meeting with my new associate I gave them a mental starching and stepped with courage into the rickety barouche that, drawn by two small and bony ponies, took us to the office of Henry W. Peabody & Co., the only American house in the Philippines.

And having entered the two upstair rooms, that looked out over the little Plaza de Cervantes, I was introduced to bamboo chairs, a quartette of desks, and half a dozen office-boys, who were rudely awakened

Our Office and the Punkah under which the Old Salts Sat for Free Sea Breezes. *See page 8.*

from their morning's slumber by the scuffle of my heavy boots on the broad, black planks of the shining floors. Across the larger room, suspended from the ceiling, hung the big "punka," which seems to form a most important article of furniture in every tropical establishment. On my arrival the boy who pulled the string got down to work, and amid the sea-breezes that blew the morning's mail about, business of the day began.

The first thing I noticed was that cloth instead of plaster formed the walls and ceilings, and seemed far less likely than the mixture of lime and water to fall into baby's crib or onto the dinner-table during those terrestrial or celestial exhibitions for which Manila is famous. For the Philippines are said to be the cradle of earthquake and typhoon, and in buildings, everywhere, construction seems to conform to the requirements of these much-respected "movers." Tiles on roofs, they say, are now forbidden, since the passers-by below are not willing to wear brass helmets or carry steel umbrellas to ward off a shower of those missiles started by a heavy shake. Galvanized iron is used instead, and, while detracting from the picturesque, has added to the security of households who once used to be rudely awakened from their slumbers by the extra weight of tile bedspreads.

And Manila houses. Down in the town, outside

the city walls, the regular, or rather irregular, Spanish type prevails, and nature, in her nervousness, seems to have done much in dispensing with lines horizontal and perpendicular. The buildings all have an appearance of feebleness and senility, and look as if a good blow or a heavy shake would lay them flat. But in the old city, behind the fortifications, are heavy buttressed buildings of by-gone days, built when it was thought that earthquakes respected thick walls rather than thin, and the sturdy buttresses so occupy the narrow sidewalks that pedestrians must travel single file. The Spanish—so it seems—rejoice to huddle together in these gloomy houses of Manila proper, but the rich natives, half-castes, and foreigners all prefer the newer villas outside the narrow streets and musty walls; and just as much as the Anglo-Saxon likes to place a grass-plot or a garden between him and the thoroughfare in front of his residence, so does the Spaniard seek to hug close to the street, and even builds his house to overhang the sidewalk. Save for carriages and dogs, the lower floors of city houses are generally deserted, and, on account of fevers that hang about in the mists of the low-ground, everyone takes to living on the upper story. Balconies, which are so elaborate that they carry the whole upper part of the house out over the sidewalk, are a conspicuous feature in all the buildings of older construction, and with their engaging overhang afford opportunities for leaning out to talk with passers-by below, or a convenient vantage-ground from which to throw the waste water from wash-basins. Huge window-gratings thrust themselves forward from the walls of the lower story, and are often big enough to permit dogs and servants to sit in them and watch the pedestrians, who almost have to leave the sidewalk to get around these great cages.

It may be just as well, before going farther, to say something about this town that is sarcastically labelled "Pearl of the Orient" and "Venice of the Far East" by poets who have only seen the oyster-shell windows or back doors on the Pasig on the cover-labels of cigar-boxes. It seems big enough to supply me with the pianos and provisions which kind friends suggested I bring out with me in case of need, and the main street, Escolta, is as busy with life and as well fringed with shops as a Washington street or a Broadway.

Spanish, of course, is the court and commercial language and, except among the uneducated natives who have a lingo of their own or among the few members of the Anglo-Saxon colony—it has a monopoly everywhere. No one can really get on without it, and even the Chinese come in with their peculiar pidgin variety.

The city squats around its old friend the river

Pasig, and shakes hands with itself in the several bridges that bind one side to the other. On the right bank of the river, coming in from the bay and passing up by the breakwater, lies the old walled town of Manila proper, whose weedy moats, ponderous drawbridges, and heavy gates suggest a troubled past. Old Manila may be figured as a triangle, a mile on a side, and the dingy walls seem, as it were, to herd in a drove of church-steeples, schools, houses, and streets. The river is the boundary on the north, and the wall at that side but takes up the quay which runs in from the breakwater and carries it up to the Puente de España, the first bridge that has courage enough to span the yellow stream.

The front wall runs a mile to the south along the bay front, starting at the river in the old fort and battery that look down on the berth where the Esmeralda lies, and is separated from the beach only by an old moat and the promenade of the Malecon, which, also beginning at the river, runs to an open plaza called the Luneta, a mile up the beach. The east wall takes up the business at that point, and wobbles off at an angle again till it brings up at the river fortifications, just near where the Puente de España, already spoken of, carries all the traffic across the Pasig. Thus the old city is cooped up like pool-balls, in a triangle three miles around, and the walls do as much in keeping out the wind as they do in keeping in the various unsavory odors that come from people who like garlic and don't take baths. Here is the cathedral—a fine old church that cost a million of money and was widowed of its steeple in the earthquakes of the '80s—and besides a lot of smaller churches are convent schools, the city hall, army barracks, and a raft of private residences.

Opposite Old Manila, on the other bank, lies the business section, with the big quays lined with steamers and alive with movement. The custom-house and the foreign business community are close by the river-side, while in back are hundreds of narrow streets, storehouses, and shops that go to make up the stamping ground of the Chinese who control so large a part of the provincial trade.

Everything centres at the foot of the Puente de España, which pours its perspiring flood into the narrow lane of the Escolta, and people, carriages, tramcars, and dust all sail in here from north, east, south, and west. As on the other side, the busy part of the section runs a mile up and down the river and a mile back from it, while out or up beyond come the earlier residential suburbs. In Old Manila, the Church seems to rule, but on this side the Pasig the State makes itself felt, from the custom-house to the governor's palace—a couple of miles up-stream.

As to population, Manila, in the larger sense, may hold 350,000 souls, besides a few dogs. Of the lot, call 50,000 Chinese, 5,000 Spaniards, 150 Germans, 90 English, and 4 Americans. The rest are natives or half-castes of the Malay type, whose blood runs in all mixtures of Chinese, Spanish, and what-not proportions, and whose Chinese eyes, flat noses, and high cheek-bones are queer accompaniments to their Spanish accents. Thus the majority of the souls in Manila—like the dogs—are mongrels, or *mestizos*, as the word is, and the saying goes that happy is the man who knows his own father.

I spent my first night in Manila at the Spanish Hotel El Oriente, and it was here that I became acquainted with that peculiar institution, the Philippine bed. And to the newly arrived traveller its peculiar rig and construction make it command a good deal of interest, if not respect. It is a four-poster, with the posts extending high enough to support a light roof, from whose eaves hang copious folds of deep lace. The bed-frame is strung tightly across with regular chair-bottom cane, and the only other fittings are a piece of straw matting spread over the cane, a pillow, and a surrounding wall of mosquito-netting that drops down from the roof and is tucked in under the matting. How to get into one of these cages was the first question that presented itself, and

Plaza de Cervantes, Foreign Business Quarter. *See page 8.*

what to do with myself after I got in was the second. It took at least half an hour to make up my mind as to the proper mode of entrance, when I was for the first time alone with this Philippine curiosity, and I couldn't make out whether it was proper to get in through the roof or the bottom or the side. After finally pulling away the netting, I found the hard cane bottom about as soft as the teak floor, and looked in vain for blankets, sheets, and mattresses. In fact, it seems as if I had gotten into an unfurnished house, and the more I thought about it the longer I stayed awake. At last I cut my way out of the peculiar arrangement, dressed, and spent the decidedly cool night in a long cane chair, preferring not to experiment further with the sleeping-machine until I found out how it worked.

Next morning my breakfast was brought up by a native boy, and consisted of a cup of thick chocolate, a clammy roll, and a sort of seed-cake without any hole in it. How to drink the chocolate, which was as thick as molasses, seemed the chief question, but I rightly concluded that the seed-cake was put there to sop it out of the cup, after the fashion of blotting-paper. Fortified with this peculiar combination, I started on my second business day by trying to remember in what direction the office lay, and wandered cityward through busy streets, often bordered with arcaded sidewalks, which were further shaded from the sun by canvas curtains.

After beginning the morning by ordering a dozen suits of white sheeting from a native tailor—price $2.50 apiece—I was introduced to the members of the English Club, and began to feel more at home stretched out in one of the long chairs in the cool library. It seems that the club affords shelter and refreshment to its fourscore members at two widely separated points of the compass, one just on the banks of the Pasig River, where its waters, slouching down from the big lake at the foot of the mountains, are first introduced to the outlying suburbs of the city, and the other in the heart of the business section. The same set of native servants do for both departments, since no one stays uptown during the middle of the day and no one downtown after business hours. As a result, on week-days, after the light breakfast of the early morning is over at the uptown building, the staff of waiters and assistants hurry downtown in the tram-cars and make ready for the noon meal at the other structure, returning home to the suburbs in time to officiate at dinner.

At the downtown club is the 6,000-volume library, and after the noonday tiffin it is always customary to stretch out in one of the long bamboo chairs and read one's self to sleep. This is indeed a land where laziness becomes second nature. If you want a book or paper on the table, and they lie more than a yard or two from where you are located, it is not policy to reach for them. O, no! You ring a bell twice as far off, take a nap while the boy comes from a distance, and wake up to find him handing you them with a graceful "Aquí, Señor!" In fact, I have even just now met an English fellow who, they tell me, took a barber with him on a recent trip to the southern provinces, to look after his scanty beard that was composed of no more than three or four dozen hairs, each of which grew one-eighth of an inch quarterly.

On the day before Christmas one of the guest-rooms at the uptown club was vacated, and I moved in. The building is about two and a half miles out of the city, and its broad balcony, shaded by luxuriant palms and other tropical trees, almost overhangs the main river that splits Manila in two. The view from this tropical piazza is most peaceful. Opposite lie the rice-fields, with a cluster of native huts surrounding an old church, while, blue in the distance, sleeps a range of low mountains. To the left the river winds back up-country and soon loses itself in many turns among the foothills that later grow into the more adult uplifts on the Pacific Coast, while to the right it turns a sharp corner and slides down between broken rows of native huts and more elaborate bungalows.

The club-house is long, low, and rambling. The reading, writing, and music rooms front on the river, and the glossy hard-wood floors, hand-hewn out of solid trees, seem to suggest music and coolness. It is possible to reach the city by jumping into a native boat at the portico on the river bank, or to go by one of the two-wheel gigs, called *carromatas*, waiting at the front gate, or to walk a block and take the tram-car which jogs down through the busy high-road.

It is very difficult to absorb the points of so large a place at one's first introduction, so I won't go further now than to speak of that far-famed seaside promenade called the Luneta, where society takes its airing after the heat of the day is over.

Imagine an elliptical plaza, about a thousand feet long, situated just above the low beach which borders the Bay, and looking over toward the China Sea. Running around its edge is a broad roadway, bounded on one side by the sea-wall, and on the other by the green fields and bamboo-trees of the parade-grounds. In the centre of the raised ellipse is the band-stand, and on every afternoon, from six to eight, all Manila come here to feel the breeze, hear the music, and see their neighbors. Hundreds of carriages line the roadways, and mounted police keep them in proper file. The movement is from right to left, and only the Archbishop and the Governor-General are allowed to drive in the opposite direction.

The gentler element, in order not to encourage a flow of perspiration that may melt off their complexions, take to carriages, but the sterner sex prefer to walk up and down, crowd around the band-stand, or sit along the edge of the curbing in chairs rented for a couple of coppers. Directly in front lies the great Bay, with the sun going down in the Boca Chica, between the hardly visible island of Corregidor and the main land, thirty miles away. To the rear stretches the parade-ground, backed up by clumps of bamboos and the distant mountains beyond. To the right lie the corner batteries and walls of Old Manila, and to the left the attractive suburb of Ermita, with the stretch of shore running along toward the naval station of Cavité, eleven miles away. To take a chair, watch the people walking to and fro, and see the endless stream of smart turn-outs passing in slow procession; to hear a band of fifty pieces render popular and classic music with the spirit of a Sousa or a Reeves, is to doubt that you are in a capital 8,000 miles from Paris and 11,000 miles from New York. Footmen with tall hats, in spotless white uniforms, grace the box-seats of the low-built victorias, while tastefully dressed Spanish women or wealthy half-castes recline against the soft cushions and take for granted the admiration of those walking up and down the mall.

The splendidly trained artillery-band, composed entirely of natives, but conducted by a Spaniard, plays half a dozen selections each evening, and here is a treat that one can have every afternoon of the year, free of charge. There are no snow-drifts or cold winds to mar the performance, and, except during the showers and winds of the rainy season, it goes on without interruption.

After the music is over the carriages rush off in every direction, behind smart-stepping little ponies that get over the ground at a tremendous pace, and the dinner-hour is late enough not to rob one of those pleasant hours at just about sunset. There are no horses in Manila—all ponies, and some of them are so small as to be actually insignificant. They are tremendously tough little beasts, however, and stand more heat, work, and beating than most horses of twice their size.

Our Christmas dinner at the club has just ended, and from the bill of fare one would never suspect he was not at the Waldorf or the Parker House. Long punkas swung to and fro over the big tables, small serving boys in bare feet rushed hither and thither with meat and drink, corks popped, the smart breeze blew jokes about, and everyone unbent.

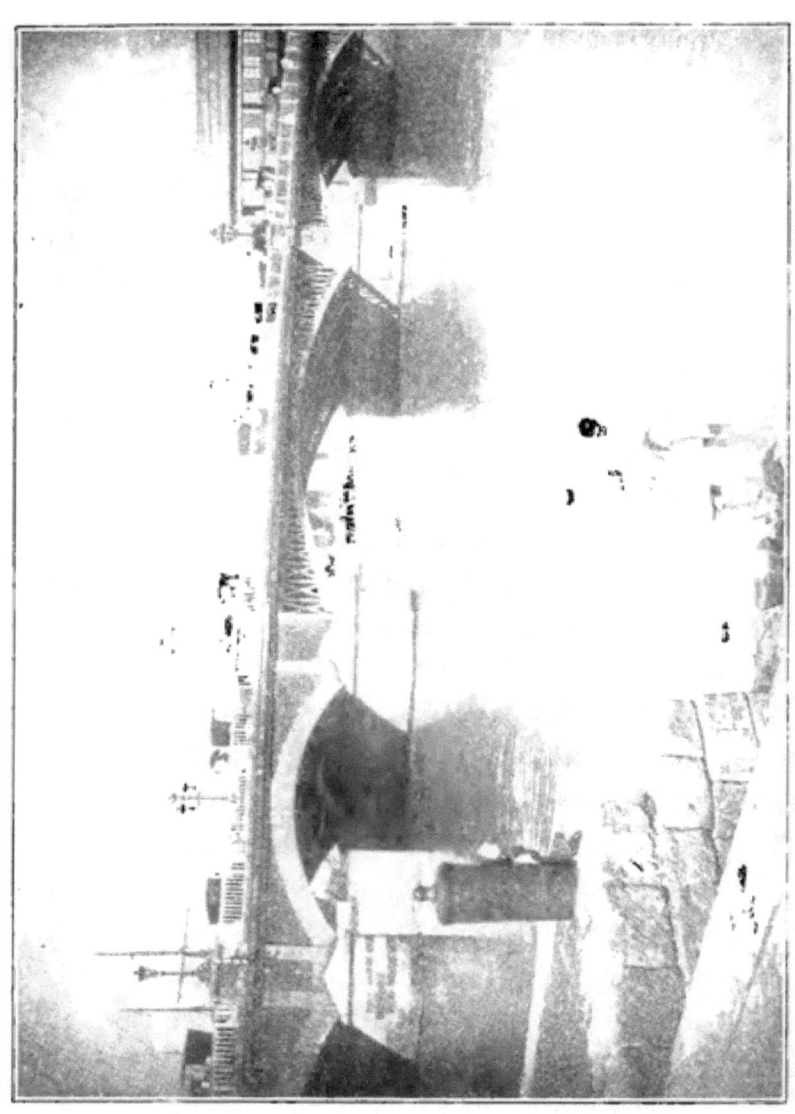

Puente de España. Manila's Main Highway Across the Pasig. *See page 12.*

Soups, fish, joints, entrées, rémoves, hors-d'œuvres, mince-pies, plum-puddings, and all the delicacies to be found in cooler climes had their turn, as did a variety of liquid courses. Singing, speeches, and music followed the more material things, and everyone was requested to take some part in the performance. By the time the show was over the piano was dead-beat and everybody hoarse from singing by the wrong method.

II

Shopping at the "Botica Inglesa"—The Chit System—Celebrating New Year's Eve—Manila Cooking Arrangements—Floors and Windows—Peculiarities of the Tram-car Service—Roosters Everywhere—Italian Opera—Philippine Music—The Mercury at 74° and an Epidemic of "Grippe"—Fight Between a Bull and a Tiger—A Sorry Fiasco—Carnival Sunday.

January 7th.

MY third Sunday in Manila is a cool breezy day, with fresh winds blowing down from the mountains. The weather has lately been as temperate as one could wish, and has corresponded to some of our soft spring conditions. From noon until three o'clock has usually seemed warm, but the mornings have made walking pleasant, the afternoons have given opportunities for tennis, and the evenings have hinted that an overcoat would not be amiss. One could hardly ask for any more comfortable place to live in than Manila as it stands to-day, and although sanitary appliances are most primitive, the city seems to be healthy and without noisome pestilence.

During the holiday season, just over, foreign business has been suspended and everyone socially inclined. Shopping has been in vogue, and on one of my expeditions for photographic materials I was introduced to the "Botica Inglesa," or English chemist's shop, which seems to be the largest variety-store in town. Here it is possible to buy anything from a glass of soda to a full-fledged lawn-mower, including all the intermediates that reach from tooth-brushes to photographic cameras.

And speaking of shopping brings me to the "chit" system, which has been such a curse to the Far East. In making purchases, no one pays cash for anything, since the heavy Mexican dollars—which are the only currency of the islands—are too heavy to lug around in the thin suits made of white sheeting. One simply signs an "I. O. U." for the amount of the bill in any shop that he may choose to patronize, and thinks no more about it till at the end of the month all the "chits" which bear his name are sent around for collection.

Result: one never feels as if he were spending anything until the first day of the incoming month ushers in a host of these big or little reminders. If your chits at one single shop run into large amounts, the collector generally brings along with him a coolie or a wheelbarrow with which to lug away the weight of dollars that you pour into his hands, and when two or three collectors come in together the office reminds one of a money-'changer's. Counterfeit money is so prevalent that one after the other of your callers bites the silver or drops it on the floor to detect lead, and to listen to the resulting sound is not to feel complimented by their opinion of your integrity. So it goes, many of the shop-keepers being swindled out of their dues by debtors who choose to skip off rather than to pay, and waking up at the end of the month to find their supposed profits existing only in the chits whose signers have skedaddled to Hong Kong or Singapore.

New Year's Eve was celebrated with due hilarity and elaborate provisions. The club bill of fare was remarkable, and when it is realized there are no stoves in Manila, the wonder is that the cooking is so complex. A Manila stove is no more nor less than a good-sized earthen jar, shaped something like an old shoe. The vamp of the shoe represents the hearth; the opening in front, the place for putting in the small sticks of wood; and the enclosing upper, the rim on which rests the single big pot or kettle. In a well-regulated kitchen, there may be a dozen of these stoves, one for each course, and their cost being only a peseta, it is a simple matter to keep a few extra ones on hand in the bread-closet. And so, as one goes through the streets where native huts predominate, he sees a family meal being cooked in sections, and is forced to admire the complexity of the greasy dishes that are evolved from so simple a contrivance.

As the Manila cooking arrangements are rude, so I suspect are the pantry's dish-washing opportunities. I really should hesitate to enter even our club-kitchen, for certain dim suggestions which are conveyed to the senses from spoons and forks, and certain plate surfaces that would calm troubled waters if hung from a ship's side, all hint at unappetizing sights. All in all, the less one sees of native cooking, *in transitu*, the greater will one's appetite be.

I had expected an early introduction to earthquakes, but none have occurred so far, and I am almost tempted to get reckless. Soon after my arrival I was inclined to put my chemical bottles in a box of sawdust, empty part of the water out of my pitcher, and pack my watch in cotton-wool in anticipation of some nocturnal disturbance. For the old stagers who saw the city fall to pieces back in the '80's deem it their duty to alarm the new arrival, and almost turn pale when a heavy dray rolls by over the cobblestones in the street near the club, or make ready to fly out-of-doors at the first suspicion of vibration.

A word or two more about the floors in Manila houses. I don't suppose there is a soft-wood tree in the islands, and as a result one sees some very interesting hard-wood productions. The floors come under this category. Rough-hewn as they are—out of huge hand-sawed hard-wood planks—they are models. By certain processes of polishing with banana leaves and greasy rags, they are made to shine like genius itself, and give such a clean, cool air to the houses that one is compelled to regard them with admiration. In fact, there is a certain charm in Manila about many specimens of hand-work that one encounters everywhere. The stilted regularities—as our good professor used to say—of machine-made articles are frequently conspicuous by their absence, and instead one sees the inequalities, the lack of exact repetition, the informality of lines that are not just perpendicular or horizontal, all of which make up the charm of work that is handmade, that reflects the movements of a living arm and mind rather than those of a wheel or a lever.

The curious windows that are everywhere are likewise instructive. Like the blinds, they slide in grooves on the railings of the balconies, and serve to shut out the weather from the interior. They consist of frames containing a multitude of small lattice-work squares, into which are placed thin, flat, translucent sea-shells which admit light, but are not look-throughable. We have all heard of shell-roads, but never of shell-windows, and one misses the presence of glass until he has got accustomed to a Manila house,

The Busy Pasig, from the Puente de España. Old Manila on the Left, Business Quarter to the Right.
See page 13.

whose sliding sides are one vast window that is rarely closed.

Manila streets, outside of the city proper, are smooth, hard, and well shaded by the arching bamboos. They are already proving attractive to the bicycle, which, though very expensive out here at the antipodes, is growing in favor, especially among the wealthier half-castes, or *mestizos*.

Tram-car service is slow, but pretty generally good. The car is a thing by itself, as is the one lean pony that pulls it. It takes one man to drive and one to work the whip, and if the wind blows too hard, service is generally suspended. The conductor carries a small valise suspended from his neck, and whistles through his lips " up-hill " to stop, and " down-hill " as the starting-sign. The usual notice, " Smoking allowed on the three rear seats only," is absent, for everyone smokes, even to the conductor, who generally drops the ash off a 15-for-a-cent cigarette into your lap as he hands you a receipt for your *dos centavos*. The chief rule of the road says:

" This car has seats for twelve persons, and places for eight on each platform. Passengers are requested to stand in equal numbers only on both platforms, to prevent derailment."

And so if there are four " fares " on the front and six on the back platform, somebody has to stumble forward to equalize the weight. No one is allowed to stand inside, and if the car contains its quota of passengers, the driver hangs out the sign, "*Lleno*" (full), and doesn't stop even for the Archbishop. It is just as well, perhaps, to sit at the front end of the car if you are afraid of smallpox, for the other morning a Philippine mamma brushed into a seat holding a scantily clothed babe well covered with evidences of that disease. One sympathizes with the single pony that does the pulling as he sees thirty people besides the car in his load, and it is no uncommon thing on a slight rise or sharp turn for all hands to get off and help the vehicle over the difficulty. The driver holds the whip by the wrong end and lets the heavy one come down with double force on the terribly tough hide of the motive power. Aside from tram-cars some of these little beasts, however, are possessed of great speed, and with a reckless *cochero* in charge, it is no uncommon sight to see three or four turnouts come tearing down the street abreast, full tilt, clearing the road, killing dogs and roosters, and making one's hair stand on end.

Speaking of roosters, they are the native dog in the Philippines. The inhabitants pet and coddle them, smooth down their plumage, clean their combs, or pull out their tail-feathers to make them fight, to their heart's content, and it is a fact that these cackling glass-eaters really seem to show affection for their proprietors, in as great measure as they exhibit hatred for their brothers. Every native has his fighting-cock, which is reared with the greatest care until he has shown sufficient prowess to entitle him to an entrance into the cock-pit. In case of fire, the rooster is the first thing rescued and removed to a place of safety, for babies—common luxuries in the Philippines—are a secondary consideration and more easily duplicated than the feathered biped. It is almost impossible to walk along any street in the suburban part of the town without seeing dozens of natives trudging along with roosters under their arms, which are being talked to and petted to distraction. At every other little roadside hut, an impromptu battle will be going on between two birds of equal or unequal merit, the two proprietors holding their respective roosters by the tails in order that they may not come into too close quarters. The cock-pits, where gatherings are held on Thursdays and Sundays, are large enclosures covered with a roof of thatch sewed onto a framework of bamboo; they are open on all sides, and banked up with tiers of rude seats that surround a sawdust ring in the centre. Outside the gates to the flimsy structure sit a motley crowd of women, young and old, selling eatables whose dark, greasy texture beggars description, while here and there in the open spaces a couple of natives will be giving their respective roosters a sort of preliminary trial with each other. As the show goes on inside, shouts and applause resound at every opportunity, and at the close of the performance a multitude of two-wheeled gigs carry off the victors with their spoils, while the losers trudge home through the dust on foot.

Other familiar street-scenes consist of Chinese barbers, who carry around a chair, a pair of scissors, and a razor wherever they go, and stop to give you a shave or hair-cut at any part of the block; or Chinese ear-cleaners, who scoop out of those organs some of the unprintable epithets hurled by one native at another. Cascades of slops not uncommonly descend into the street as one walks along beneath a slightly overhanging second story of some of the houses, and one is impressed, if not wet, by this favorite method of laying the street-dust.

Besides the daily afternoon music on the Luneta, a full-fledged Italian opera troupe has come to town and has begun to give performances in the Teatro Zorilla. "Carmen" and "The Cavalleria Rusticana" are on the bill for this week, and many other of the old standbys are going to have their turn later.

In respect to music, sidetracked though it is, Manila seems to be more favored than her sister capitals in the Far East, and everyone appears to be able to play on something. Such of the native houses as are too frail to support pianos shelter harps, violins, and other stringed instruments, while some of the more expensive structures contain the whole selection. Of an evening—in the suburbs—it is no uncommon thing to hear the strains of a well-played Spanish march issuing from under the thatch of a rickety hut, or to find an impromptu concert going on in the little tram-car which is bringing home a handful of native youth with their guitars or mandolins. Every district has its band, some of the instruments in which are often made out of empty kerosene-cans, and the nights resound with tunes from all quarters. In fact, the Philippine band is one of the chief articles of export from Manila, and groups of natives with their cheap instruments are shipped off to Japan, India, and the Spice Islands, to carry harmony into the midst of communities where music is uncultivated. All in all, it is extremely curious that out of all the peoples of the Far East the Filipinos are the only ones possessing a natural talent for music, and that the islands to-day stand out unique from among all the surrounding territory as being the home of a musical race, who do not make the night as hideous with weird beatings of tom-toms as they do poetic with soft waltzes coaxed from gruff trombones.

January 18th.

Manila is pretty well, thanks. The weather has been cool and comfortable. Showers have come every day or two to lay the dust, and one could not want a more salubrious condition of things. The sunsets from the Luneta have been more than pyrotechnic, and I now believe that nowhere do you see such displays of color as in the Orient, Land of the Sunrise. During these three weeks of my stay, so far there have been five holidays, and we have had ample time to take afternoon walks up the beach, or play tennis at the club, or indulge in moonlight rows on the Pasig.

A week ago on the island just opposite the club, where lies a good-sized village, containing an old church, there was a religious festival, which lasted all the week. This was the Fiesta of Pandacan, and all the natives for miles around came pouring down by our veranda, in bancas and barges, on their way across the river. Every night during the week, bands of music played on one side of the stream and on the other side, and then crossed to their respective opposites, playing *in transitu*, and then setting up shop on shore again. Then there were fireworks, bombs, and rockets galore, so that the early night was alive with noise and sparks. On the evening of the grand windup we crossed over to see the sights, in one of the usual hollowed-out tree-trunk ferryboats. Crowds of

A Philippine Sleeping-machine. *See page 14.*

gayly dressed natives surged around the plaza, near the old church, while everywhere along the edges squatted old men and women, cooking all sorts of greasy "chow" on those peculiar Philippine stoves described in the last chapter. Everybody smoked, as well as the pots and kettles, and the air was therefore foggy. The little, low-thatched houses were jauntily decorated with lanterns and streamers, and at all the open fronts leaned out rows of grinning natives.

Here and there were small "*tiendas*," or little booths, where cheap American toys, collar-buttons, pictures, and little figures of the Saviour were sold, and great was the hubbub. The houses, as well as the people, are very low of stature, and as we walked along the narrow, almost cunning streets, our shoulders level with the eaves of many of the shanties, and above the heads of many of the people, we felt indeed like giants. Many were the pianos in those native huts, and peculiar mixtures of strikingly decent playing fell upon the ear from all sides.

The whole circus wound up with a grand pyrotechnical illumination of the old church from base to tower, and a score of loud explosions, caused by the setting off of many dozen bombs at the same time, made up in noise what the religious celebration lacked in spirituality. Then all the bands came back and played their lungs out as they crossed the river, and all the people rushed for bancas, and came chattering home. Thus did this pretty little religious show consume, in noise and sparks, the contributions of a very long time.

The grand opera company which is here is doing remarkably well, and "Faust" was given the other evening to a crowded house. The theatre Zorilla is round, like a circus, and in the centre of the ring sit the holders of our regular orchestra seats, facing the stage, which chops off the segment of the circle opposite the main entrance. In a rim surrounding the central arena stretches the single row of boxes, a good deal like small open sheep-pens, separated from each other only by insignificant railings. Next comes the surrounding aisle, and in the broad outside section of the circle, rising up in steep tiers, are the seats for the natives and gallery gods, who invariably bring their lunch with them, to pass away the time during the long intermissions. The orchestra is a native one, led by an Italian conductor, and doesn't tuck its shirt into its trousers. The musicians, who battle with the difficult score, grind out their music quite as successfully as some of our home performers, who would scorn the dark faces and flying shirt-tails of their Philippine brethren.

During the performance the management introduced a ballet, whose members were native Filipinas. It was too laughable. The faces and arms of the women who formed the corps seemed first to have been covered with mucilage, and then besprinkled with flour in order to bring the dark-brown complexion up to the softer half-tints of the Italian performers. The native lady, as a rule, is unacquainted with French shoes or high heels, slippers being the every-day equipment, and when these flowery beings came forward on to the stage, saw the huge audience, and tried to go through the mazes of the dance in European footgear, they felt entirely snarled up, even if they didn't look more than half so. But this only served to keep the audience in a good humor, and everybody seemed to enjoy both the singing and the deviltry of *Mephistopheles*, whose part was well taken. The waits between the acts were long, and the drop-curtain was covered with barefaced advertisements of dealers in pills, hats, and carriages. But there were cool little cafés across the roadway running by the theatre, and one forgot the delay in the pleasure of being refreshed by Spanish chocolate and crisp *bunuelos*.

In front of the main entrance to the theatre stood two firemen, with hose in hand, ready to play on anything as soon as the orchestra stopped or a lamp fell, but otherwise nothing was particularly strange.

The whole structure was oil-lighted with rickety chandeliers, which shed a dangerous though brilliant glare down upon a large audience of most exquisitely dressed Spanish people, *mestizos* and foreigners. Pretty little flower-girls wandered about trying to dispose of their wares to the rather over-dressed dudes of the upper half-caste 400, and their mammas often followed them around to assist in making sales. If it begins to rain in the afternoon, before the performance, everybody understands that the show is to be postponed, provided clearing conditions do not follow, and those who hold tickets are, as a rule, grateful not to be obliged to risk their horses and their starched clothes to the treatment of a possible downpour.

The Luneta is still a close rival to the opera, and each afternoon a dozen of us will generally meet there to refresh ourselves with the music and the passing show. Toward sundown, in the afternoons, of late, the big guns in the batteries up along the walls of Old Manila, hard by, have been used in long-distance sea target-practice, and it has been interesting, on the way from the office to the promenade, to walk along the beach and see the cannon-balls zip over the water and slump into it miles from their destination. The same target serves every afternoon, and seems perfectly safe from being hit. I wish I could say as much for the fleet of American ships that are lying off the breakwater, at the anchorage.

February 8th.

It seems peculiar to see the moon standing directly overhead o'nights, and casting a shadow of one's self that is without meaning. I never yet realized we had so little shape before, looking from above, as when I saw this new species of shadow the other night, and was really sorry that the angels never had a chance to look at us from a better point of view.

To be politic, and begin with the weather as usual, a cold snap lately has given everyone the "grippe." The mercury actually stood at 74° all one day, and couldn't be coaxed to go higher. Think of the suffering that such low temperature would occasion among a people who have no furnaces or open fireplaces. You may think I am facetious, but 74° in the Philippines means a great deal to people who are always accustomed to 95°.

The opera-talk continues, and "Fra Diavolo" was most successfully performed to a crowded house the other evening. "The Barber of Seville" was given Sunday night with equal *éclat*, and the *prima donna* was a star of the first water, whose merits were recognized in the presentation of some huge flower-pieces, probably paid for by herself. But the opera has had a rival, and those who are not so musically inclined have spent most of their spare moments in discussing the great bull and tiger fight which took place Sunday afternoon.

It was a queer show, and not altogether edifying. The old bull-ring, squatting out in the rice-fields of Ermita suburb, was to be used for the last time, and the occasion was to be of unusual interest, since the flaming posters announced, in grown-up letters:

STRUGGLE BETWEEN WILD BEASTS.

Grand Fight to the Death between Full-blooded Spanish Bull, and Royal Bengal Tiger, Direct from the Jungles of India.

For days before the show came off, conversation in the cafés along the Escolta invariably turned to the subject of the coming exhibition, and it was evident that the managers fully intended both to reap a large harvest of heavy dollars and to wind up the career of the bull-ring association in a blaze of blood and glory.

The steaming Sunday afternoon found everybody directing his steps toward the wooden structure which consisted of a lot of rickety seats piled up around a circular arena. The reserved sections were covered with a light roof, to keep off the afternoon sun, but the bleaching-boards for those that held only "*billetes de sol*" were exposed to the blinding glare. The audience, a crowd of three thousand persons, with dark faces showing above suits of white sheeting, found the centre of the ring ornamented with a huge iron cage some two rods square, while off at the sides were smaller cages containing the "*fieras*," or wild beasts.

The show opened amid breathless excitement, with an exhibition of panthers, and a man dressed in pink tights ate dinner in the big cage, after setting off a bunch of firecrackers under one of the "*fieras*," who didn't seem inclined to wake up enough to lick his chops and make-believe masticate somebody. The daring performer lived to digest his glass of water, with one cracker thrown in, and a deer was next introduced into the enclosure. The panther, at command of the keeper to get to business, seemed unwilling to attack his gentle foe, and on continued hissing from the big audience, the two animals were at length withdrawn.

Then great shouts of "El toro! El toro!" arose, as off at the small gate, at one side, appeared the bull, calmly walking forward, under the guidance of two natives, who didn't wear any shoes. And renewed applause arose, as the small heavy cage containing the R. B. tiger was rolled up to a sliding-

door of the central structure. The bull was shoved
into the iron jail, the gate closed, a dozen or more
bunches of firecrackers were set off in the small box
holding the tiger, in order to waken him up, the
slide connecting the two was withdrawn, and, with a
deafening roar, the great Indian cat rushed forth and
tried to swallow a man who was standing outside the
bars waving a heated pitchfork. The bull stood
quietly in one corner wagging his tail, and after
blinking his eyes once or twice, proceeded to examine his antagonist, in a most friendly spirit. In
fact, there seemed to be no hard feeling at all between the two beasts, and the tiger only wanted to
get at the gentleman outside the cage, not at the
bull. The audience howled, jeered at the tiger, bet
on the bull, and criticised the man with the pitchfork as he gave the tiger several hard pokes in the
ribs. This served to anger the beast so that he
finally did make a dive at the bull, and promptly
found himself tossed into the air. But as he came
down, he hung on to the bull's nose, and dug his
claws into the tough hide. Curiously enough, the
bull didn't seem to mind that in the least, and the
two stood perfectly still for some five minutes, locked
in close quarters.

To make a long story short, there occurred four
or five of these mild attacks, always incited by

The English Club on the Banks of the Pasig. A *Banca* in the Foreground. *See page 16.*

the man with the pitchfork, during which the bull stepped on the tiger, making him howl with pain, and the latter badly bit the former on the legs and nose. After the fourth round, both beasts seemed to be in want of a siesta. It was growing dark, and the dissatisfied audience cried for another bull and another tiger. The first animal was finally dragged away, after the tiger had retreated to his cage, and a fresh bull with more spirit was introduced. Now, however, the tiger was less game than ever, and no amount of firecrackers or pitchforkings could induce him to stir from the small cage. He seemed far too sensible, and literally appeared to be the possessor of an asbestos skin.

It had now got pretty dark, and the audience joined in the pandemonium of howls coming from the various cages. People began to light matches to see their programmes, and the circus-ring looked as if it were filled with fireflies. Then the programmes themselves were ignited for more light, and cries of "Give us back our money," "What's the matter with the tiger?" and others of a less printable order, arose. Men jumped into the ring, but the tiger refused to move for anybody. In the hope of stirring things up, a couple of panthers were again hastily wheeled up and pushed into the cage, where the bull was standing with an expression of wonder on his face. But the bull merely licked one panther on the nose and wagged his tail at the other, while the show was declared off on account of darkness. Then everybody filed out in disgust, and the man with the tiger, panthers, and pitchfork made arrangements to sail for foreign shores by the first steamer. Such was the last performance in the Plaza de Toros de Manila.

It was a pleasant contrast after the fight to adjourn to the Luneta. The day was Carnival Sunday, and all the young children of the community were rigged up in many sorts of inconceivable gowns. Clowns and ballet-dancers, devils and angels, all wandered up and down the smooth walk, and the crowd was immense. Numbers of the older people also took part, and many of the smart traps were occupied with grotesque figures. The artillery-band rendered some of its finest selections. The ships off in the bay were almost completely reflected in the calm water. The mountains rose blue, like velvet, in the distance, and a red glow in the Boca Chica told where the sun had gone down for us, only to rise on the distant snows of New England.

III

A Philippine Valet—The Three Days Chinese New Year—Marionettes and Minstrels at Manila—Yankee Skippers—Furnishing a Bungalow—Rats, Lizards, and Mosquitoes—A New Arrival—Pony-Races in Santa Mesa—Cigars and Cheroots—Servants—Cool Mountain Breezes—House-snakes—Cost of Living—Holy Week.

February 16th.

NEWS to begin with. I have engaged a Philippine valet, price $4.50 per month; a man with a wife, two children, and a fighting-cock, who buys all his better half's pink calico gowns and all the food for the party on this large salary. It is a wonder what revolutions have taken place in my wardrobe. My heavy clothes, already grown musty from disuse, have been taken out, sun-dried, and laid carefully away. I no longer have to decide what to wear each morning, for it is settled for me beforehand. Everything that my "boy" wishes me to don is laid out on a chair during my early pilgrimage to the bath, and all that is necessary to do on my return is to get into them. It is quite a luxury, and I shall certainly be inclined to bring this cheap gentleman back with me when I return to Boston. My neckties, which have hitherto snarled themselves up in the corner of a drawer, now are hanging from a neat clothes-line, side by side. My books and papers on the centre table are arranged with unnatural formality, and the smaller articles, such as lead-pencils, buttons, pin-cushions, are all adjusted in definite geometrical formation. At breakfast and dinner in the club-house I no longer have to whistle to be waited on, for my slave is always behind the chair, ready to spill the soup on my coat or pass the plum-pudding. These serving-boys all belong to the Tagalog race, which seems to include in its numbers most of the native inhabitants in Manila and the adjacent towns. They all have straight, thick black hair, speak their peculiar Tagalog language, and only pick up enough Spanish to carry them through the performance of their simple duties.

And still the holidays, more or less, continue. About this time of year there is one a week, and just now the Chinese New Year occupies about three days. The business part of the town is quiet. All the Chinese merchants have driven off on a picnic, and it is impossible to hire carriages of any sort.

Manila, on the whole, is waking up, and besides the opera we now have the marionette troupe, something entirely new to the average citizen. It seems there are four sisters travelling around the world with their little collection of string-pulled puppets, giving exhibitions in all the larger centres. Their fame had preceded them, and so the other night when the doors of the Teatro Filipino were thrown open, a huge crowd assembled to see the performance. The stage was a fairly large one, but so arranged optically that it made the figures appear larger than they really were. The actors (puppets) were remarkable for their lifelikeness, and if one had not seen the strings stretching upward he would have taken them to be animate beings. Their costumes were complete and elaborate in every particular. First came a tight-rope walker, then an acrobat balancing a pair of chairs, and then Old Mother Hubbard, out of whose voluminous petticoats jumped half a dozen little men and women, all of whom danced and cut up as if they were really reasoning bipeds instead of material, loose-jointed, wax-faced dolls. Old Mamma was especially good, and as she stirred up her little children with a long staff, looked at first this one and then that, shook her head, pointed her finger, and danced with the others, she brought down the house with applause.

Later on came a minstrel troupe, with two end-men, a leader who waved a baton, a harpist, and two other musicians. They all played, and the end-men cracked jokes. Next came a clog-dance between two darkies, and it was difficult to believe that they were not alive. Further on came a bulldog, which grabbed a policeman by the nether breeches and pulled a huge piece out of them; a bull, who chased a farmer and threw him over a rail fence (this took wonderfully well, for the Spaniards go crazy over anything with a bull in it); then a boarding-house scene, with a folding-bed that shut up its occupants inside; next, a balloon ascension, in which a man on the ground was suddenly caught up into the air by an anchor thrown out from the balloon; then the death of the two aëronauts, who fall from a dizzy height; next, a ride in a donkey-cart by two lovers, who find themselves run away with and get snarled up on the wagon, to be kicked black and blue by the donkey. Finally came a very complete little play of "Bluebeard," with complete scenery, costumes, and ballet. All of the scenery was of the lightning-change sort, and the Spaniards, *mestizos*, and natives in the audience sat and looked on with open-mouthed wonder, too astonished to laugh, too senseless to cry, and able but to clothe their faces with expressions of wonder.

To change the subject rather abruptly, the captain of the Esmeralda, the little steamer on which I came from Hong Kong, has been good enough to ask me on board his vessel to tiffin as often as she comes into port. As Captain Tayler's table is noted both for its excellence and profusion, the very few of us who comprise the American colony, as well as all the

The Bull and Tiger Fight—Opening Exercises. *See page 38.*

Englishmen in town, always covet an invitation to spend Sunday in his company and enjoy various dishes that are not to be procured in Manila markets.

Besides the several steamers that ply between ports on the neighboring coast, there is now a large fleet of American ships at anchor in the bay, and our office, which shelters the only American firm in the Philippines, is a great centre for the various Yankee, nasal-twanged skippers, who, dressed in hot-looking, ready-made tweeds, come ashore without their collars to ask questions about home topics and read newspapers six weeks old. They delight to enjoy the sea-breezes generated by our big punka, and only leave the office on matters of urgent necessity. Several of the captains have their whole families with them, and one, who is especially well-to-do, owns his own ship, carries along a bright tutor, who is preparing some of the skipper's sons for college, and has transformed the vessel into a veritable institution of learning. On nearly every evening the whole fleet in a body go to some one ship, sing songs and have refreshments, and the other night Governor Robie was the host. Being invited to partake of the festivities, we two Yankees went off into the bay at about sunset, ate a regulation New England dinner, with rather too much weight to it for hot climates, and met all the belles of the fleet. The moon overhead was full, and with a good piano, violin, hand-organ, and a couple of ocarinas, giving vent to sweet sounds, we had an impromptu dance on the quarter-deck. We stayed out on the ship of our host and hostess all night. They apologized because the bunks in the state-rooms assigned to us were so hard, little realizing that we couldn't sleep worth a continental on account of their being so ridiculously soft after our Philippine cane arrangements.

Everybody is talking horse now, and business will be at a standstill during the first few days of the coming month, when the pony races take place at the suburban course in Santa Mesa. As a result, every afternoon that some of us do not go rowing or play tennis, we adjourn to the race-track, and, in company with groups of Spaniards and wealthy *mestizos*, watch the smart ponies circle around the track.

And, speaking of the race-course, I have just made arrangements with one of my new friends to take a bungalow situated on a low rise that backgrounds the track at the quarter-mile post. It stands, prettily shaded by bamboo-trees, on practically the first bit of upland that later grows into the lofty mountains of the interior, and the view off over the race-course and low-lying paddy-fields, squared off into sections, toward the city, is most picturesque. On another side we look off over the winding river toward the mountains, which hardly appear five miles away, and still another view is a bamboo grove, against which is backed up our little stable with various outbuildings, including the kitchen. A broad veranda runs entirely around the main building, where the living-rooms are located, and Venetian roll-blinds let down from the piazza-roof keep off the afternoon sun.

Yesterday I had my first experience in making extensive purchases of furniture, and was interested to see about twelve coolies start off from the city toward our country residence, three miles away, loaded down with beds, tables, chairs, and other articles. Four of them started off later on with the upright piano balanced on a couple of cross-sticks resting on their shoulders, and trotted the whole distance without sitting down to play the "Li Hung Chang March" more than twice. These living carriers rather take the place of express wagons in the East, and a long caravan of furniture-laden Celestials, solemnly going along through the highway at a jog-trot, is no uncommon sight. We shall need dishes, knives, pots and kettles, and a whole World's Fair of trumpery, before we get started, and I shall have to be busy with a Spanish dictionary, in order to get familiar with the right names for the right things.

You have asked me how the mosquitoes fare upon the newly arrived foreigner. To tell the truth, I have not seen more than half a dozen since coming to Manila, and those all sang in tune. Everybody sleeps under nettings, of course, but so far I have not seen as many biters flying around at night as there are in the United States of America. To be sure, one sees a good many lizards hanging by the eye-teeth to the walls, or walking about unconcernedly up-side-down on the ceilings, but they do good missionary work by devouring the host of smaller bugs, and it is one of our highest intellectual pursuits here in Manila to stretch out in a long chair and go to sleep gazing upward at these enterprising bug-catchers pursuing their vocation. And, now and then, from some piazza-roof or ceiling will drop on your face a so-called hairy caterpillar whose promenade on one's epidermis will cause it to swell up in great welts that close one's eyes and ruffle the temper.

Rats are more numerous than mosquitoes, and the other day, on my opening a drawer in some of our office furniture, three jumped out. The office was transformed into an impromptu race-course, and all hands were called to take part in the slaughter. But Manila doors are loose-jointed, and the rodents escaped somewhere into the next room. Since then I have had the legs sawed off of my desk, so that these literary beggars, who delight to eat up one's valuable papers, should not climb in and make a meal off of my private cable code—a thing which they started to do some time ago. They have already several times run off with the candle which was used for heating sealing-wax, and possess such prowess that they even took it out of the candlestick.

We had a new arrival at the club lately in the person of a young Englishman who came fresh from Britain. Someone had stuffed him with tales of indolent life in the Far East, for he came in to his first dinner at the club clad only in pajamas and green carpet-bag slippers. He also thought that the Spanish language consisted in adding final a's to words in the English tongue and shouted all over the club next morning for sopa, sopa, with which to cleanse himself. But the servant brought him a plate of soup, and he is now trying to remember that soap in Spanish is translated by *jabon*, not sopa. *Jamon*, the word for ham, however, is close enough to give him trouble and he will no doubt ask for soap instead of ham at our next repast.

March 16th.

The pony races came off with great *éclat* on the first four days of this month, and were decidedly interesting. All Manila turned out, and such a collection of carriages I have never seen. All the Spanish ladies put an extra coat of paint on their complexions, and, dressed in their best bibs and tuckers, made somewhat of a ghastly show in the searching light of early afternoon. The high, thatched-roofed grand stand presented a duly gay appearance as the bell rang for the first event, and the dried-up paddy-fields, far and near, crackled with natives directing their steps toward the centre of attraction.

In front of the grand stand groups of Spaniards, Englishmen, and sea-captains formed centres for betting, and off at the sides were refreshment-booths to which everyone made pilgrimage as often as the articulatory muscles were in need of lubrication.

Some of the ponies were splendid-looking little "critters" and made almost as fast time as their larger brethren, the horses. During race-afternoons, business in the city was entirely suspended, and everyone who had a dollar took it to the race-course to gain other dollars. As the currency system is all metal, bets were paid in hard coin, and if you happened to buy a lucky ticket in that gambling machine, the "totalizator," you would perhaps have a whole hatful of heavy silver cartwheels shoved at you on presenting the winning pasteboard. And it was no uncommon sight at the close of the races to see some of the thinly clad natives whom fortune had favored go trudging home across the rice-fields, carrying a load of dollars in a straw hat or a bright bandana.

One by one the vessels are dropping away from their anchorage in the bay, and by Saturday our Vigilant will heave up anchor and start on her twenty-thousand-mile journey to Boston via the Cape, with her big cargo of hemp. Thanks to our attentions to the captains, they have seemed willing to take home for us any amount of souvenirs and curios, and I have sent along quite an assortment of stuffed bats, lizards, and snake-skin canes, which I feel sure will cause somebody to creep on their arrival.

Manila's best cigar, made of a special, selected tobacco, wrapped in the neatest of silverfoil and packed in rosewood boxes tied with Spanish ribbon, costs about five cents and is considered a rare delicacy. One scarcely ever sees these cigars, the "Incomparables," outside of the city itself, and the brand is so choice that but few smokers are acquainted with it. The foreigner in Manila thinks he is paying dear for his weed at $20 per thousand, and some of our professional smokers limit themselves to those favorite "Bouquets" which correspond to our "two-for-a-quarter" variety but sell here for $1.80 a hundred. Below these upper grades come a various assortment of cheaper varieties, including the cheroots, big at one end and small at the other, and the $3-a-thousand

cigars which are made of the first thing that comes
handy, to be sold to the crews of deep-water mer-
chantmen. A native of the Philippines wants his
cigarette, and gets it. Packages of thirty are sold
on almost every corner for a couple of coppers, and to
my mind the Manila cigarette is far superior to the
variety found in Cuba. Smoking is, of course, encouraged by prices such as these, and one finds it
perfectly good form to borrow a cigarette, as well as
a light, from his neighbor in the tram-car or on the
plaza. Even on the toll-bridge which spans the Pasig
you pay your copper for crossing, and get in change
a box of matches; and if you are queer enough not
to want the matches, the man will give you instead a
ticket that avails for the return trip.

Sunday I left my room at the club and moved into
our new house out in the suburb of Santa Mesa. It
is just a week now since the Chinese cook came and
began to christen the pots and saucepans, whose
Spanish names I shall never get to remember. He
began by rendering me a small account of the
"extras" provided for our table, and I was floored
the first thing on an item of five cents put down as
"Hongos." I asked him what that was. He spluttered
around in Spanish and looked about the room to
see if he couldn't find a few growing in one of our
pictures of still life on the walls. At length, being

Suburb of Santa Mesa. From the Veranda of our Bungalow We Looked down on the Rice-fields and Race-course. *See page 48.*

struck with an inspiration, he seized a small fan, excitedly stuck it into one of our flower-pots, balanced on top of it an inverted ash-tray, and danced around, pointing first to the item on the bill and then to the peculiar growth in the flower-pot. I confess I didn't follow his reasoning, till suddenly it struck me that for our first dinner in the new house we had partaken of mushrooms. Not far off from an ash-tray balanced on a Japanese fan growing out of a flower-pot—are they? The style of decoration in our house is especially Japanese, and, needless to say, artistic, since there are large Japanese and Indian shops in Manila, where one can get all sorts of gimcracks at low prices. Our servants number seven, a small quota for two of us. Although their wages are small, amounting, as a rule, to $4 apiece per month, yet it is necessary to have plenty of them, in order that a certain few shall be awake when wanted.

The fresh breeze, which in the evenings and early mornings blows down direct from the lofty mountains, is so cool that often several blankets have been necessary in the sleeping contrivance. Mosquitoes are still conspicuous by their absence, but the rats up in the roof sound tremendously numerous. All night they seem to be pulling boxes to and fro, taking up boards and nailing them down, and having a general all-hands-round sort of a dance.

Nearly all of the older bungalows in Manila possess what are called house-snakes; huge reptiles generally about twelve or fourteen feet long and as thick as a fire-engine hose, that permanently reside up in the roof and live on the rats. These big creatures are harmless, and rarely, if ever, leave their abodes. Judging from the noise over my cloth ceiling, a pair of these pets find pasturage up above, and I can hear them whacking around about once a week in their chase after rats. They are good though noisy rat-catchers, but since they must needs eat all they catch, their efficiency appears to be limited to their length of stomach, and one night of energetic campaign is generally followed by several days of rest, during which the snake sees if he has bitten off more than he can chew. If the Philippine cats were more noble specimens of the quadruped, I should try to place half a dozen up in this midnight concert-hall, but they are so feeble that I fear their lives would be in danger. It is hardly to be wondered at that these native cats are modestly retiring, when you wake at night to hear your shoes being dragged off across the floor by some huge rice-fed rodent, and I don't blame them at all for having right angles at the end of their tails.

The only way to get rid of the rats seems to be to buy more snakes, and this is simple enough, for you often see the natives hawking them around in town, the boas curled up around bamboo poles, to which their heads are tied.

Some of our other domestic pets are lizards, supposed to be about four feet long, who sing every evening at 8.30 P.M., from somewhere off down in the shrubbery; several roving turkeys and pigs that belong to the boys that serve us, a cluster of fighting-cocks, and a family of puppies. It is easy to be seen that our establishment is thus somewhat of a tropical menagerie, and a performance is almost always going on in some quarter or other.

I have just completed the purchase of a horse and carriage complete, including the coachman, for $100, and on the first trial we passed everything on the road. The pony is a high-stepper, and rattled along over the ground at a terrific speed, as a good Philippine animal should. The coachman seems to know how to drive, which is a rare attainment among the natives, and so far, though he has run over two boys, he has not taken off any wheels in the car-tracks.

They say it costs a good deal to live well out this way, but that is a mistake, and if one lived at home in the same style the bills would be at least ten times as large. To be sure, it would be possible to come to Manila, board with a Spanish family in the old city, avoid joining the club, and live almost for nothing. However, this is a custom not much encouraged in the Orient, and one cannot properly take his place among the colony of English and other Europeans without spending a certain reasonable amount.

Business is done more on a social scale than at home, and the lowest English clerk in the large houses feels that he must enter into the free and easy expenditure of his better-paid chief. After office hours are over everyone stands on the same social plane, and all business talk is tabooed. The office-boy often calls his lord and master "Bill," and frequently has a better-looking horse and carriage.

The U. S. S. Concord has just come into the bay and been saluted by the fort. Some of her officers will probably come ashore to breakfast at the club, and it will probably devolve on the four Americans in the city to do what is needful in the way of courtesy to our fellow-countrymen.

To-day is the beginning of Easter Week, nearly all of whose days are holidays or holy days. This is one of the closest-observed seasons of the year, and on next Thursday and Friday, if you will believe it, no carriages are allowed to appear in the streets either of Manila or of the other cities. The tram-cars, to be sure, have of late years been allowed to run, and the doctor's carriage and the ice-carts can obtain permits. Beyond them, however, everybody has to stay at home or walk; and in former times tram-cars were forbidden and no one was allowed to carry an open umbrella. It seems the proper thing to do to make arrangements with some of the English colony to take a trip off into the mountains, and my chum and I expect to start off by launch on Wednesday afternoon. Our party will consist of five, not including half a dozen servants, who are to make arrangements for bringing the provisions and bedding.

On my return I hope to have some fodder for my pen and relate some of our experiences in the up-country districts.

IV

An Up-country Excursion—Steaming up the River to the Lake—Legend of the Chinaman and the Crocodile—Santa Cruz and Pagsanjan—Dress of the Women—Mountain Gorges and River Rapids—Church Processions—Cocoanut Rafts—A " Carromata " Ride to Paquil—An Earthquake Lasting Forty-five Seconds—Small-pox and other Diseases in the Philippines—The Manila Fire Department—How Thatch Dealers Boom the Market—Cost of Living.

March 27, 1894.

THE Easter holidays have come and gone, and one of the favorite vacation trips from Manila has been brought to a close. Five of us have seen lake, mountain, and river scenery; have been taking interesting walks, drives, swims; have camped out in a good house and enjoyed the hospitality of our native Indian friends. Whistling for the punka-boy to go ahead, I will now set down the record of our trip.

The week from the 18th of March to the 25th was practically one long holiday, but it was Wednesday, the 21st, in the afternoon, that we left Manila for the interior. Rand and I got up the trip by procuring a large and commodious steam-launch for five days — gratis. Having done our share, we left our three companions to look after the " chow " and

Our Destination Was a Town Called Pagsanjan at the Foot of a Range of Mountains. *See page* 63

other kindred topics. To my "boy" I merely said, "Wednesday we are going up to the laguna; prepare what is necessary for four days." That was all, and on Wednesday afternoon I found him at the launch with my clothes and bedding all ready to start. Here also were assembled hams, boxes of ice, and other provisions, big bundles of personal effects, and the four "boys" (a "boy" may be seventy years old if he likes) whom we were going to take along.

The whistle blew, the special artist with his camera ambled aboard, amidst a pile of sun-hats, oranges, and excitement, and soon the Vigilante was steaming up the river on her sixty-mile trip. Familiar objects were first passed, but soon after leaving the up-town club new scenes presented themselves. The launch stirred up large waves astern that washed both banks of the river with great energy, and the first incident was the swamping of three banca-loads of grass that were on their way down to Manila under charge of Indian pedlers. Turn after turn opened up new scenes; our house on the hill began to fade away, and soon we skimmed through native villages where white blood was "not in it." The hills increased in size, the river lessened, and great bamboo-trees hung over toward the central channel. At one point, high up on the bluffs, perched a Chinese pagoda-like chapel, said to have been constructed by a wealthy Celestial as a thanks-offering for his escape from a crocodile. He was bathing in the river, so the story goes, when suddenly he saw the monster making for him. He threw up his hands and vowed to build a monument to his patron saint if escape was vouchsafed him. And no sooner had he spoken than the crocodile turned to stone and lies there to-day, a long, low black mass, fretting the current that ripples over it. As we passed the rock it looked as if it had never been anything else, but the afternoon was too pleasant to doubt the veracity of the legend. On we went. The mountains ahead grew more to look like masses of rock and trees and less like soft blue velvet. Pasig, an important town, was left behind, the lowlands came again, a multitude of fish-weirs stuck up ahead, and before we knew it the great lake was holding us on its rather muddy waters just where it slobbered into the mouth of the river, its only outlet.

On all sides save the one by which we had entered rose the mountains right out of the water, and I was reminded of Norway or Scotland. It was like a sea, and the farther shore was below the horizon. The sun had set and the full moon rose just ahead as we kept along the coast to the north. At half after eight o'clock we anchored off a little town called Santa Cruz that seemed to be backed up by two very lofty mountain-peaks, and we were soon surrounded by two *bancas* filled with natives who began to transfer our many effects. And so we left the launch, were slowly poled ashore, and next found ourselves on a sandy beach surrounded by much people and baggage. Dispatching two of our retinue up into the town to fetch enough of the two-wheeled covered gigs called *carromatas* for our assembly, in about three-quarters of an hour we had the felicity of seeing seven come racing down the road to the lake shore. Our destination, by the way, was a town called Pagsanjan, about three-quarters of an hour from Santa Cruz, and situated just at the foot of a range of mountains. The chattels were soon loaded, there was a cracking of whips, a creaking of harness, and the long procession started off at a rattling gait through the town and out into the rich cocoanut groves beyond.

At Manila, outside of bamboo and banana trees, there is no sign of really equatorial vegetation, but up in the mountains there was no deception, and Nature did her best to let us know that the temperate zone was far away. We bounced along at a terrific pace and presently saw the lights of our little village. Rattling through an old stone archway, we drew up before the house of a certain Captain Feliz, to whom we had been recommended. The genial old man, whose face and corporosity were charmingly circular in their rotundity, welcomed us with open-armed hospitality, and saying he knew of just the house that would accommodate our party, started to lead us to it. After a few steps he suddenly stopped, apologized smilingly, said he had forgotten his set of false teeth, and must return for them. And coming back shortly after, he took out his teeth, commented on their grace and usefulness, and said he could speak much better Spanish with than without them.

In due season we drew up at a very thick-walled stone house on the high bank just above the river, and were invited to take possession. Our "boys" got out the provisions in short order, for a late supper; our pieces of straw matting were spread out around the edges of the shining floor of the large "*sala*" which had been placed at our disposal for a dormitory; pillows and light coverings were duly regulated, and after eating a bit, we said good-night to our new friends and turned in on the floor to rest. I found the hardwood planks so soft after my bed at Manila that before long I arose, arranged eight chairs in facing pairs, spread out my sleeping-arrangements, and soon fell asleep in a very good improvised bed which was high enough from the floor to keep cockroaches from using me as a promenade. Thursday morning we arose early, washed ourselves on the balcony that overlooked the fashionable avenue of the village, and, as is the true Philippine custom, sprinkled the street with solutions of soapsuds.

Now, as I have said before, the Thursday and Friday before Easter are tremendously sacred days in the Philippines, and no carriages of any description are permitted to move about. The little town was still as death, and the early-morning hush was only broken now and then by the weird caterwaulings of the peculiar Passion songs which the natives in these parts sing off and on during Lent. Later on, as we finished breakfast, groups of women began coming out of the various houses and directed their steps churchward. Most of them were gorgeously dressed in all colors of the solar spectrum—with a little cloth added on—and it was instructive to see an expensively gowned Indian woman emerge from a shabby little *nipa* hut that didn't look as if it could incubate such starched freshness. For the dresses that some of these people wear are costly; and even their *piña* neckerchiefs often cost $100.

After breakfast we went down to the river and got into five hollowed-out tree-trunks, preparatory to the start up into the mountain-gorges. It was worse than riding a bicycle, trying to balance one of the crazy affairs, and for a few moments I feared my camera and I would get wet. However, nobody turned turtle, and we were paddled up between the high cocoanut-fringed banks of the wonderfully clear river before the early morning sun had looked over the mountains into whose cool heart we were going.

Then came the first rapids, with backgrounds of rich slopes showing heavy growths of hemp and cocoa palms. Another short paddle and the second set of rapids was passed on foot. A clear blue lane of water then stretched out in front of us and reached squarely into the mountain fastnesses through a huge rift where almost perpendicular walls were artistically draped with rich foliage that concealed birds of many colors, a few chattering monkeys, and many hanging creepers. Again it seemed like a Norwegian fjord or the Via Mala, but here, instead of bare rocks, were deeply verdured ones. Above, the blue sky showed in a narrow irregular line; below, the absolutely clear water reflected the heavens; the cliffs rose a thousand feet, the water was five hundred feet deep, the birds sang, the creepers hung, the water dripped, and we seemed to float through a sort of El Dorado, a visionary and unreal paradise. At last we glided in through a specially narrow lane not more than fifty feet wide; a holy twilight prevailed; the cliffs seemed to hold up the few fleecy clouds that floated far over our head, and we landed on a little jutting point for bathing and re-

Where the Crackers were Wet. The Rapids in the Gorges of Pagsanjan.
See page 67.

freshments. It seemed as if we were diving into the river Lethe or being introduced to the boudoir of Nature herself. In an hour we pushed on, passed up by three more rapids, and halted at last at the foot of a bridal-veil waterfall that charmed the eye with its beauty, cooled the air with its mists, and set off the green foliage with its white purity. Here we lunched, and in lieu of warm beer drank in the beauties of the scenery.

The return was a repetition of the advance, except that we shot one or two of the rapids, and that the *banca* holding the boy and the provisions upset in a critical place, wetting the crackers that were labelled "keep dry." We got back to our house by early afternoon, and all agreed that an inimitable, unexcelled, wouldn't-have-missed-it-for-the-world excursion had passed into history.

Good old Captain Feliz took us to call on some of the native villagers in the late afternoon, who exhibited quite a bit of Indian hospitality. At one house was a pretty Indian girl who spoke Spanish very well and entertained our party of six with as much grace as an American belle. Of course the presence of five "Ingleses" in town was quite an event in a place fifty miles from Manila, and as we walked through street after street each house-window presented at least seven curious faces; dogs barked, fighting-cocks crowed, and the occupations of the moment were suspended.

After dinner we sat out on the balcony to watch the procession that wound around through the various streets, starting from the fortress-like church and finally bringing up there. These church parades are a good deal like our torch-light processions, except that here images, not mud-besprinkled men, carry most of the torches. In this affair there were a dozen or more floats, each one bearing a saint, an apostle, or somebody else, and each decorated with very costly drapery, ornaments, and elaborate candelabra illuminators. Scattered all along between the floats straggled natives carrying poles on which were images of a candle, a hand, a spear, a pair of nails, a cock, a set of garments, and other symbolic articles relating to the crucifixion. Then came Peter on a very elaborate moving pedestal, and in his hand he held the traditional bunch of keys. Then a Descent from the Cross, with two apostles standing up on step-ladders. Next came the band of the procession —three men singing to the tune of an old violin—and finally the Virgin Mary with glass tears rolling down her wax cheeks. On each side of the line from start to finish trooped the populace, mostly women dressed in black and carrying candles.

Next day was Good Friday. No traps of any description to be had, as none were allowed to run, and so we spent the day about the town and in walking up into the hills. A look into the great, solid old church in the morning showed us a fragrant and gaudily dressed audience kneeling in various postures on the tiled floors, while numerous dogs of various cross breeds and tempers meandered in through the door and among the worshippers. From the church we strolled across a very primitive bamboo bridge over a branch river, and wandered through a luxurious cocoanut grove beneath whose tall trees were situate a couple of very rudimentary cocoanut-oil mills and the houses of the operators. The machinery was very crude. One might think he was back in the days of stone knives, seeing these simple contrivances, the awkward levers, the foot-power grindstones, and the old pots and kettles. In the river near the mills were thousands of cocoanuts ready to be tied together in rafts for floating down to Manila, and everybody's business up this way seemed to consist in watching this oily fruit fall from the trees.

In the early evening, just before another religious procession started, we heard a great clatter up in the belfry of the old church, and learned that the hubbub was made by "devil-frighteners." On inquiring as to the nature of this weird clap-trap symphony, it seems that on these especially holy days men are stationed up in the bell-towers with huge wooden rattles, which they so manipulate from time to time that the noise is said to act as a scare-crow to the various devils who are supposed to be hovering about seeking whom they may devour.

After another peaceful night's rest, some of us took our morning jump into the river, and all prepared for a twelve-mile *carromata* drive out along the lake shore beneath the mountains, to a little village called Paquil, said to be possessed of a crystal spring bathing-pool. The road for a good bit of the way was of the Napoleon-crossing-the-Alps style, and it got to be so bad I rather thought we were in for a walk. Not a bit of it. The *carromatas* are built strong as the rocks themselves, the wheels are huge and solid, the ponies tough as prize-fighters, and the driver urges the whole affair along at a tremendous pace. So we bounced along, and most of our time was spent, not on the seat, but midway between it and the roof, which occasionally came down and thumped our heads. On the way we passed through numerous little villages, and in one out-of-the-way place we called on an American, Thomas Collins, who has been practically shut in out here for twenty-five years. It seems that he got cheated out of a hundred and fifty thousand dollars' worth of valuable wood a good while ago by the officials of a certain provincial district, and has been trying to get the claim paid ever since. He was a queer chap, and had almost forgotten how to speak American; but at last he managed to remember the word "hell," and then his ideas began to flow more freely.

When we arrived at Paquil our conductor, the genial Captain Feliz, walked up to the house of an acquaintance and asked him to put it at our disposal. As before, the request was father to the grant, and we dumped our chattels down into a parlor full of wax virgins and crucifixes. The bath, for which the village is quite famous, is a large pool five feet deep, with a pebble bottom. At one end a stream of clear water gushes forth from the hillside, while at the other an overflow brook carries off the surplus and goes bubbling down through the village to the lake. We had our swim after all the native bathers had left, and got back to our house in time for a tiffin that had been brought with us in the baskets. In the early afternoon we took our siesta, in the later hours started for our jogglety return drive, and at Pagsanjan found prepared for us a feast of sucking pigs.

On Sunday morning we were ready for our return to Manila. The seven gigs arrived, we said hearty farewell to our friends, presented Captain Feliz some empty bottles and two teapots, and rattled out through the town toward Santa Cruz, where our launch was in waiting. The trip was cool and pleasant across the lake, but it was hot when in about four and a half hours we got to the low river-country again. The sail down was like the sail up, and by dinner-time we backed water to bump into the portico of the club, where all hands disembarked for dinner. Thus ended what I suppose is the most popular and most delightful excursion which the foreigner can make from the capital of the Philippines in the few days which the church feasts at Easter put at his disposal.

April 6th.

The other night I dreamt I was climbing up a long hill on a bicycle. Once at the top, I started down over the other side at a terrific pace. Somehow or other, by mistake, the wheel ran off into a gutter at the side of the road, and bounced around in such a dangerous manner that it all but upset. However, with tremendous exertion, I managed to jump the mechanism back onto the smooth ground again, and continued safely down to the bottom of the hill at a two-forty gait. Arrived at the bottom, I conveniently woke up, and heard a rat under the bed trying to slide one of my shoes off across the floor.

Next morning, on coming down to the office, several of my business friends asked me if I had felt the severe

Cocoanut Rafts on the Pasig, Drifting down to Manila. *See page 69.*

earthquake shock during the night. I said "No," and inquired as to the particulars. It seems that the shock lasted some forty-five seconds, and my chum was awakened by his bed commencing to rock around and by the four walls of his room attempting to move in different directions. Nothing in the city was much injured, I believe, and next day the really excellent observatory, conducted by the Jesuits, gave out a full illustrated description of the affair.

Up at our new bungalow, the only incidents worthy of note have been the attempted stealing of my pony and the consumption of my best shoes by one of our house-rats.

A Philippine burglar, curiously enough, takes off his clothes, smears his dark skin with cocoanut-oil, and prowls around like a greased pig that cannot be caught. One of these slippery thieves got into our stable, unhitched my pony, and took him almost to the front gate before the sleepy coachman found his wits. But prompt action saved the day, and the lubricated robber escaped, leaving his booty pawing the ground.

But with my shoes I was not so fortunate. I woke up suddenly to hear something being dragged across the floor. Thinking it was only a rat making off with a boot-jack with which to line his nest, I refrained from tempting Providence by leaving the protection of the mosquito-netting. Next morning I found that one of these rodents had pulled a pair of my patent-leather shoes off a low shelf beneath the bed, dragged them out into the hallway behind a hat-rack, and eaten up the most savory portions of the bindings. Complimentary to the prowess of the rat or to the lightness of my shoes—which? I keep them now as articles on which the patent has run out—worthless, but curiosities.

Otherwise things have run smoothly, and each evening we lie in the long chairs on the broad veranda, watching the Southern Cross come up over the hills, or the score of brush-fires of dried rice-stalks that illuminate the darkness away off toward the mountains. The music from our piano seems to give much delight to the members of the servants' hall, now nine in number, besides several puppies and game-cocks. The other night, although in the midst of the hot season, we had a prodigious cold snap again, when the thermometer went down to sixty, after being ninety-five during the day, and two blankets were not at all uncomfortable.

I see by the papers that there are at least two cases of small-pox in Boston, that everybody is alarmed and hundreds are getting vaccinated. Curious state of affairs—isn't it?—when every day out here you see small children running around in the streets, covered with evidences of this disease. Nobody thinks anything about small-pox in Manila, and one ceases to notice it if a Philippine mamma sits opposite you in the tram-car, holding in her lap a scantily clothed child whose swarthy hide is illuminated with those unmistakable markings. Some weeks ago there were even four hundred deaths a week in Manila from this disease alone; and from the way in which the afflicted mix with the hale and hearty, you can only wonder that there were not four thousand. But small-pox flourishes best in the cool, dry days of our winter months, and is now being stamped out by the warmer weather. An effort is being made to have everybody vaccinated, and the steamers from Japan have brought down whole cargoes of lymph, but the natives do not see any reason why they should undergo this experiment, and would much prefer to have the small-pox than to be vaccinated. And this being the case, it is no wonder that almost seventy-five per cent. of them bear those uncomplimentary marks of the disease's attention.

Now that I have inoculated my page with a reference to this rather unpleasant subject, it is only a bit of sad truth to tell of the only fatality caused by the malady in our little Anglo-Saxon colony. Recently I went into the Bay with a young Englishman who had always lived in terror of this one disease, and had avoided both contact with the natives and excursions into the infected districts. The launch took me to the vessel which we were loading, and then carried him on to that receiving cargo from his concern. Later she returned with him, picked me up, and together we went ashore to stop a moment at the club before going home for the day. I never saw him again, poor chap, though I did take over his stable, for next morning he was taken with black small-pox and died in a week.

The families of the lightermen in the Bay—crowded as they are into the hencoops over the stern of the bulky craft—are full of it, and hence the fatal ending to our little afternoon excursion. As a rule, however, the members of the English-speaking colony get so used to this disease that they have no especial fear in suddenly turning a sharp corner of running into some native sufferer.

In days gone by, when cholera decimated Manila's numbers, when people died faster than they could be buried, when business was at a standstill and the city one great death-house, were the times that tried men's souls. But now that those big water-mains which run along the ground bring fresh water from far up into the hills, the natives have given up the deadly practice of drinking from the river, and, thanks to the good supply system, no longer give the cholera free admittance.

Besides small-pox, then, fever is about the greatest enemy, and certain types of the malarial variety seem so common that the sufferers from them often walk into the club, drop into a chair, and say, "Got the fever again. Means another lay-off." If they can keep about, the old stagers never give up; but novices buy thermometers and cracked ice, and either go through a terrific siege, like my friend, whose eight weeks' struggle shrunk his head so that in convalescence his hat touched his ears, or escape with a week's initiation. Typhoid seems also common, and there is generally one member of the colony, for whom the rest are anxious, stretched out in icebaths and wishing he had never seen the Philippines. The old hands—who, by the way, seem to be regular sufferers from the fever—all say the only way to be safe is to drink plenty of whiskey, but so far I have found that the less one takes the better off he is.

Someone in the States has suggested that if things get too hot it would be well to run over to Hong Kong for a change of scene. But if there is any place in the world that is hotter, stickier, more disagreeable than Hong Kong, in the months from May to October, let us hear from it. It is far worse in summer than Manila, for, completely shut in as it is by the mountains, it does not receive the benefit of the

southwest monsoon, which blows with great force
over the Philippines during the above months. Even
Japan itself gets a good roasting for the two or three
months of the hot season, and there is not much left
to do but to seek cold weather in Australia. Our only
very hot months here are said to be April and May;
sometimes part of June. The sun now is directly
overhead and going fast to the north of us, but so far
the temperature has never been unbearable. The mercury stands at about ninety-five from twelve to three
each day, but somehow or other one does not feel it
so much in the cool white suits, unless he attempts to
fall asleep on some of the sheet-iron roofs. The
nights are still cool and comfortable, and what with
a cold snap now and then, such as I spoke of above,
fans are having a poor sale. In the afternoon, walking, rowing, and tennis are still possible, and the
bands of the Luneta still have enough wind left to
give us the "Funeral March" or "Prize Song."

April 28th.

Manila fare, like Manila life, is not unwholesome,
but it lacks variety, and one rather tires, now and
then, of soup, chicken, beefsteak, and toothpicks—
four staples. But fortunately for us who like variety,
though unhappily for five or six hundred other people,
there occurred a vast conflagration yesterday after-

The Little Native School under the Big Mango-tree. *See page 92.*

noon that sent about five or six hundred houses sailing off through the air in the form of smoke.

As we were getting ready to leave the office for the day, clouds of smoke suddenly began to rise over the iron house-roofs to the eastward, and we knew that one of Manila's semi-annual holocaustic celebrations was in progress. The church bells began to ring, and all sorts of people and carriages started toward the centre of interest.

The Manila Fire Department consists of about six hand-engines and a few hose-carts, and if a fire gets started it generally burns along until an open field, a river, or a thick mass of banana-trees stops its progress. The English houses, to be sure, have recently gotten out from home one of their small steam "garden-pumps," and many of the young Britons have had weekly practice in manipulating its various parts. When the alarm for the present fire rang you might have seen several servants, employed in their respective homes by the members of the new Volunteer Fire Department, slowly wandering toward the shed where the engine was kept, with some nicely folded red shirts, coats with brass buttons, helmets with Matterhorn-like summits, and axes that shone from lack of work. These youths did not seem to be in any hurry, and it turned out that when they reached the engine-house, when their masters had togged up sufficiently well to impress the spectators, and when the engine finally got to the fire, the buildings had been translated into their new and rather more ethereal form.

The fire was two miles, more or less, from the centre of the town. The Volunteer Fire Brigade had to haul the engine the entire distance, as they feared that if the usual *carabao* oxen were hitched on, the speed over the pavements would be too great. After reaching the centre of action, an hour was spent in waiting for the man who brought some spare coal in a wheelbarrow and in choosing a location which would not be uncomfortable for the brigade. Consequently, the "London Garden Pump" was stationed to windward of the fire, on a side where it could not possibly spread any farther, and thus all stray flames and smoke were avoided. A hose was stuck down into the creek, and steam turned on. A stream of water about large enough to be clearly visible with a microscope suddenly jumped forth into the middle of the street, wetting the spectators. Somebody had forgotten to attach the extra pieces of hose that were to lead down to the fire, and steam had to be turned off. After everything was ready to get to business, a tram-car came along, and it wasn't allowable to stop its progress by putting a hose across the track, even if there was a fire. And so it went from grave to gay, the swell brigade furnishing the humorous part of the otherwise rather sad spectacle.

A Philippine fire is like any other, except that with the many *nipa* houses it does its work quickly and well, and in this instance the whole affair lasted but a couple of hours. Hundreds of families moved out into the wet rice-fields, with all their chattels, and there were many curious-looking groups. In saving various articles of furniture and other valuables, the fighting-cock, as usual, was considered the most important, and it was interesting to watch the natives trudging along with scared faces, holding a rooster by the legs in one hand and a baby or two in the other. Pigs, chickens, and dogs seemed to come next in value, and after them ice-chests and images of the Virgin Mary. The sun went down on a strange spectacle, and it was hard not to pity all the crowd that were thus rudely thrown out of their habitations. Myriads of spectators there were and myriads of carriages, of all ages and sizes, some loaded with chattels ready to take flight, and others waiting to be. At dusk, however, all danger was over; the mobs departed north, east, south, and west; the brigade carefully brushed the dust off their boots and shirts, and the poor burned-out unfortunates looked with moistened eyes on the ruin of their homes.

The wags go far enough to say that the dealers in

thatch are responsible for many of the big fires both in the capital and smaller villages and that, when times are bad or prices for thatch low, they arrange to "bull" the market by means of a conflagration. A lamp is tipped over—a thousand houses go up in smoke, and as go the houses so rise the prices for *nipa* thatch.

The second series of pony races occurred during the middle days of this month, at the race-track down below our bungalow, and all Manila again came rolling up through the dust to see the performances of the smart ponies. The events were but a repetition of those which took place in March, except that in many respects the running-time was better and the races far more close and interesting.

Some of the old stagers are beginning to complain of the heat. We take afternoon tea now and then, as is customary in all the business houses, with some of our friends, in an office on the other side of our building. Yesterday afternoon a thermometer placed outside of our window registered 125° F., I suspect this was owing to some of the reflected heat coming from the iron roofs. Inside the room the mercury stood at 97° F., but we drank our hot tea and enjoyed the coolness which resulted from consequent perspiration.

I have now been settled in Manila long enough to

find out what it costs to live, and the general cheapness of existence is more appalling than I first thought. Our house is a good one, with all the comforts of home, and is surrounded by an acre or two of land. We have stables for our horses and outbuildings for the families of our servants. At the end of the month all expenditures for house-rent, food, wages, light, and sundries are posted together and divided by three, and with everything included my monthly share comes to twenty-nine gold dollars— less than one of our American cart-wheels—*per diem.*

Where in the States could you rent a suburban house and lot, keep half a dozen servants, pay your meat bill, your drink bill, and your rent all for less than a single dollar a day! You can scarcely drive a dozen blocks in a hansom or buy a pound of Maillard's for that money at home and yet, in Manila, that one coin shelters you from the weather, ministers to the inner man, and keeps the parlor in order.

Our cook, for instance, gets forty cents each morning to supply our table with dinner enough for four people, and for five cents extra he will decorate the cloth with orchids and put peas in the soup. To think of being able to get up a six-course dinner, including usually a whole chicken, besides a roast, with vegetables, salad, dessert, fruit, and coffee, for such a sum seems ridiculous in the extreme.

The methods of marketing are almost as noteworthy as the low prices for "raw materials." All meat must be eaten on the same day it is killed, since here in the tropics even ice fails to preserve fish, flesh, or fowl. As a result, while the beef and mutton are killed in the early morning—a few hours before the market opens—the smaller fry, such as chickens and game, are sold alive. From six to ten on any morning the native and Chinese cooks from many families may be seen bargaining for the day's supply among the nest of stalls in the big market. After filling their baskets numbers of them mount the little tram-car for the return trips to their kitchens and proceed to pluck the feathers off the live chickens or birds as they jog along on the front or rear platform. By the time they have arrived home the poor creatures are stripped of foliage, and, keenly suffering, are pegged down to the floor of the kitchen to await their fate. Then, when the creaking of the front gate announces the return of the master, it is time enough to wring the necks of the unfortunates and shove them into the boiling-pot or roasting-pan that seems but to accentuate a certain toughness which fresh-killed meat possesses.

The washing-bill, again, is far from commensurate with the fulness of one's clothes-hamper, and for two gold dollars per month I can turn over to my laundry-

Calzada de San Miguel, Cooled by Fire-trees and Bordered with Residences of Rich Europeans.
See page 96.

man—who comes in from the country once a week—as much or as little as I please. Two full suits of white sheeting clothes a day for thirty days make one item of no mean dimensions, and yet the *lavandero* turns up each week with his basketful, perfectly satisfied with his remuneration. Then, too, he washes well, and although, when I see him standing knee-deep in the river whanging my trousers from over his head down onto a flat stone, I fear for seams and buttons, nothing appears to suffer. And although he builds a small bonfire in a brass flat-iron that looks like a warming-pan and runs it over my white coats all blazing as it is, the result is excellent, and one's linen seems better laundered than in the mills that grind away at home.

As servants, these boys of ours could teach much to some of their more civilized brethren from Ireland or Nova Scotia now holding sway in American families. They take bossing well, and actually expect to have their heads punched if things go wrong. They don't put their arms akimbo and march out of the house if we mildly suggest that the quality of ants in the cake or the water-pitcher is not up to standard, and actually make one feel at liberty to require anything of them.

And speaking of ants, these little creatures are everywhere ready to eat your house or your dinner right from under you. The legs of the dining-table, the ice-chest, and the sideboard must be islanded in cups of kerosene, and even the feet to one's bed must undergo the same treatment, in order that the occupant may awake in the morning to find something of himself left. Cockroaches are almost equally fierce and, endowed with wings, these creatures, sometimes four inches long, go sailing out the window as you close your eyes and try to step on them. They prowl around at night, with a sort of clicking sound, seeking something to devour, and are apparently just as satisfied to eat the glue out of a book-cover as they are to feed on the rims to one's cuffs or shirt-collars, moist with perspiration.

What the ants don't swarm over the cockroaches examine, and what they reject seems to be taken in charge by the heavy green mould that beards one's shoes, valise, and tweed suits at the slightest suggestion of wet weather.

V

Visit of the Sagamore—Another Mountain Excursion—The Caves of Montalvan—A Hundred-mile View—A Village School—A "Fiesta" at Obando—The Manila Fire-tree—A Move to the Seashore—A Waterspout—Captain Tayler's Dilemma—A Trip Southward—The Lake of Taal and its Volcano—Seven Hours of Poling—A Night's Sleep in a Hen-coop.

May 9, 1894.

THE other day the yacht Sagamore dropped anchor in the bay, her owner and his guests, all Harvard men, having got thus far on their tour around the world. I was sitting on the Luneta, Sunday evening, when I saw those familiar Harvard hat-ribbons coming, and in behalf of our little American colony welcomed the wearers of them to Manila. In return for a dinner or two at the club and a visit to the huge cigar-factories, where three or four thousand operators pound away all day at the fragrant weed, I spent a noon and afternoon aboard the yacht, glad to enjoy a change of fare. The Sagamore is a worthy boat and seems to be loaded up with gimcracks and curios of all classes and descriptions. A collector would positively be squint-eyed with pleasure to see the old vases, carved wood-work, plaques, knives, sabres, pots and kettles that her passengers have picked up all along the way; and it is indeed the only method by which to scour curios from the Orient. The boys thought the Luneta was the best place in its way they had yet seen, and it was as much as I could do to get them away from listening to the artillery-band and looking at the crowds of people in carriages. Three men in a boat of the Sagamore's size make a pretty small passenger-list for a pretty long voyage.

We've kept up our record as tripsters by having gone again up into the mountains, seen pounds of scenery, breathed fine air, and received great hospitality from the natives. Monday was a bank-holiday, so late on Saturday afternoon four of us started in two-horse *carromatas* for a mountain village called Montalvan, about twenty miles from Manila. Two boys had been sent along a day ahead, with provisions and bedding, to find a native hut and provide for our arrival. We had a delightful drive out of Manila, passed through numerous native villages, forded three rivers, saw a fine sunset, and at about eight o'clock, after a three hours' journey, pulled up at a little native house situated in a village at the foot of a lofty mountain-range. The occupants seemed willing and glad to turn out of their little shanty and put it at our disposal, and we were very comfortable. The house was not large, but it had a very neat little parlor—curious name for a room out here—and in the corner, covered with a light bed-quilt, stood a wax figure of the Virgin Mary, with the usual glass tears running down her cheeks. The family of about fourteen slept somewhere out in the rear regions of the building, leaving us to spread out around the floor of the little *sala*, like unmounted club sandwiches.

One of the party, more sensitive than the rest, woke about one in the morning and disturbed us by finding some four-inch spiders stringing cobwebs from the end of his nose to his ear and down to one finger. He was for the moment embarrassed enough to shout for joy and throw his slippers somewhere. But except for this, and a few rats that now and then tickled our toes, we slept well, and next morning before breakfast we went down to the shallow river for a swim. After a jolly good bath, a hearty breakfast, and a few preparations, our party of four, with the two boys and two guides, started up a steep valley that wound in among lofty mountains to the so-called Caves of Montalvan.

One of our guides was the principal of a village school, who held sway over a group of little Indian girls under a big mango-tree, and he shut up shop to join our expedition.

In about two hours and a half our caravan reached the narrower defile that pierced two mountains which came down hobnobbing together like a great gate, grand and picturesque. From a large, quiet pool just beneath the gates, we climbed almost straight up the mouth of the stalactite caves that run no one knows how far into the mountains, starting at a point about two hundred feet above the river. The guides made flare-torches of bamboos, and we entered the damp darkness, bounded by white limestone walls from which hung beautiful stalactites that glistened as the light struck them. In we went for a long way, now crawling on hands and knees and now stumbling into large vaulted chambers. Blind bats flew about and water trickled. It was ghostly, uncanny, but interesting. It seemed as if we were going into the very heart of the mountain, or were reading "King Solomon's Mines," and this impression was further carried out when we came to a small subterranean river that coursed down through a dark outlet and disappeared with weird gurglings. Unpleasant but perhaps imaginary rumblings suggested that a sudden earthquake might easily block our exit, and, retracing our steps, we breathed more freely on coming to the first glimmer of light. Once more in the air, we descended, took a good swim in the pool, lunched, and lay around for an hour. After another bath later on, we donned our sun-hats and trudged homeward over the long, rough path. A good walk, a good supper, a little

A Native Village Up Country. *See page 70.*

dancing and music by the natives who occupied our house, and we went to sleep upon the floor.

Next morning, after another early bath in the river, our party started to climb the mountain back of the town for a little experience in the bush. The work was hard and warm, but at the top came the reward of a superb view for a hundred miles around. Manila and the great plain, the bay and mountains beyond, were glorious before us, and behind the great mountain wilds that reached to the Pacific stretched off and up in great overlapping slabs of heavy greenness.

The plain was cut up into the regulation checkerboard farms of the richest looking description, and the scene was very much like an English one. Far away at the edge of the Bay could be seen the glistening white houses and steeples of Manila. Away to the northwest and southwest were the great fertile stretches of country that produce tons and tons of rice and sugar, reaching to the sky or distant mountains. We had luncheon in a leafy grotto; the guides found water, and brought it in lengths of bamboo which they cut down; deer ran past now and then down below us, and a short siesta on a bed of leaves finished off our morning's work. The return was so steep that it seemed as if we should go heels over head. However, we hung on to the long grass, and painted our once white suits with dust in the effort to reach level ground again. After a long descent, we came to the big mango-tree where the rural school was in session, and the little Filipinos were immediately given a recess. They rushed about, got benches and water for us, and the old schoolmaster, who had left his wife to do the teaching while he went with us, set two or three of the shavers at work mopping off his ebony skin. Our visit at the school was in the order of an ovation. The children opened their almond eyes almost to the extent of turning them into circles, and when the camera was pointed at them for the first time in their young lives, their mouths so far followed suit that recitations had to be suspended.

After thoroughly disorganizing discipline in the establishment, we accompanied the half naked president of the seminary—who had been our guide—to the river, and there washed off such of the day's impressions as went easily into solution.

And finally, after returning to our hut for tea, we packed up our baskets, whistled for the *carromatas* and jolted back to Manila through a flood of dust and sunset.

Although the hot season is trying to do its best to scorch us, it has but dismally succeeded, and we have had scarcely any severe weather at all. The thunder-showers, harbingers of the southwest monsoon and the wet season, began two weeks ago, and it rains now nearly every afternoon. The nights are all delightfully cool, and a coverlet is always comfortable. The sun is going well to the north to make hot June and July days for people in the States, and our season of light is growing shorter. When he gets back overhead again, heavy clouds will protect us from his attentions.

Owing to the outbreak of black plague or something else among the Chinese in Hong Kong, the quarantine regulations here in Manila will cause the steamer by which I was going to send the mail to miss connections. It was at first reported there were three thousand deaths in Hong Kong in six days, but I believe they have now taken off one or two ciphers from that amount. At all events Manila seems to be below the zone of this peculiar epidemic and is much better off at this time of the year than Hong Kong, which swelters away in that great unventilated scoop in the mountains.

The men of the big artillery-band that plays at the Luneta twice a week have all been vaccinated lately, and are too broken up to blow their trumpets. The people are objecting, because the infantry band doesn't make nearly as good music, and only plays twice a week at most. The third regimental band is still fighting the savage Moros with trombones down at the south, although it is rumored they will soon return, and so at present about all the music and fireworks we have are derived from the thunderstorms that play around the sheet-iron roofs as if they meant business. But in spite of the terrific cannonade of sound and the blinding flashes of lightning nothing seems to get hit, and the iron roofs may act as dispersers of the electric fluid even though attracting it.

June 6th.

Several days ago, a number of us went up the railroad line to see a "fiesta" at a little village called Obando. It was a religious observance lasting three days, and pilgrims from many villages thought it their duty to go there on foot. A great dingy old church with buttressed walls yards thick, a large plaza shaded by big trees, and beyond, on all sides, the native houses. Such a crowd I have rarely seen. Everybody seemed to think it his duty to dance; and men, women, old men and children, mothers with babies and papas with kids, shouted, jumped around, danced, joggled each other, and rumpussed about until they were blue in the face, dripping with heat, and covered with dust. Then they would stop and another crowd take up the play. As the circus proceeded the crowds increased; the old church was packed with worshippers who brought candles, and, receiving a blessing, spent an hour or so on the stone pavements in positions of contrite humility. Around the walls of the church were placed realistic paintings of the chromo order, representing hell and the river Styx, and as the natives looked at portraits of devils driving nails into the heads of the tormented, of sulphurous flames that licked the cheeks of the wicked in this world, or serpents that twined themselves into square knots around the chests of a dozen unfortunates, and of countless horned demons who plucked out the heartstrings of the condemned, they counted their beads with renewed vigor and mumbled long prayers.

Countless little booths stood like mushrooms round about outside, and cheap jewellery, made in Germany, found ready sale. The dancing and shouting increased as the sun sank in the west, until the ground fairly shook and the dust arose in vast clouds. Around the edge of the church, under the porticoes, slept sections of the multitude who were preparing themselves to take part in the proceedings when others were tired out. It was a motley crowd, a motley scene, and an unforgettable collection of perfumes.

We left after a few hours' stay, and got back to Manila to find water a foot deep in some of the streets, as a result of one of the tropical thunderstorms which have now begun in real earnest. And speaking of rain, everything is looking fresh and green, now that the dusty days of the hot season are a thing of the past. All the bamboo-trees have leafed out anew, flowering shrubs have taken life, and all nature seems to have had a bath.

One of the most showy trees in Manila is the *arbol de fuego* (fire-tree) and this product of nature resembles a large oak in general and a full-blown Japanese cherry blossom in particular. Many of the streets in the city are bordered with groups of these fire-trees, of large and stately dimensions, and at present they are simply one mass of huge flaming red blossoms growing thickly together and showing a wonderful fire-like carnation color. Scarcely any leaves make their appearance on these trees during the season of blossom, and although now and then bits of green look out from the mass of red, yet the general effect is a vast blaze of burning color.

We have left our country house on the hills of Santa Mesa, and have moved down to a little villa on the seacoast. The third man of our party, like many of his brother Englishmen who are burdened with small salaries but large debit balances, has at last decided to save money and room at his office. The house had too many regular boarders in the form of rats and snakes, was too large and too far off for the two of us left, and we decided to make a move to the seashore district. Our army of servants successfully solved the transportation problems involved, and we are now settled in new quarters. Although we miss the view of the mountains, and even the paddy-fields, we now get the salt air first hand, look out over the waters of the Bay, and are lulled to sleep by the rhythmic beating of the waves on the beach. Our view seaward leads the eye across a beautiful garden belonging to one of the rich house-owners living directly on the shore front, and the green of the trees, with the scent of somebody else's flowers, temper both the excess of glare and the brackish qualities of the sea-breeze.

In Malate, where we now are, things are much civilized. We find we miss the snakes in the roof, but we have running water in the house and a shower-bath in the bath-room; two rooms on the first floor; a parlor, two bed-rooms, dining-room, large hallway, kitchen, bath and "boys'" rooms on the second floor; a small garden at the front and a stable at the back, and all included in a rent of $15 a month. The stable accommodates two ponies, and it is a jolly drive down-town in the morning or home in the evening. The road leads all the way along by the sea, Luneta, and Malecon Promenade, that runs under the yawning mouths of the old muzzle-loaders in front of the grim walls of the old city, between

them and the beach. The salt-water bath in the
early morning is often very pleasant, though the temperature of the liquid is somewhat too high to be
exhilarating. Now and then some of the Britons
living in the neighborhood will issue a summons
for a sunrise swimming-party, and one of them will
perhaps punctuate the ceremonies by supplying a
typical breakfast of fresh fish and boiled rice, on
the veranda of a house that perhaps overlooks the
Bay. These seaside houses are particularly cool
and fresh now that the winds of the southwest monsoon come blowing into the front windows directly
off the water, but later on, when typhoons become
epidemic, it looks as if we should have the wind in
more than wholesale doses.

June 12th.

Although the San Francisco steamer does not sail
for Hong Kong until the 21st, it is necessary, on account of this quarantine business, to post our letters
in the Manila office to-day.

Two of our latest vessels have come in together and
begun to take in their cargoes of hemp for Boston.
The captains are ruddy-faced veterans who seem to
have taken part in the Civil War. One of them, who
wears false teeth when he is ashore, and hails from
New Hampshire, is particularly fond of cooling off
under our big punka. The other may be of French

A "Chow" Shop on a Street Corner. Stewed Grasshoppers for a Penny.

descent, though he comes from Ireland, and looks something like one of our distinguished Boston statesmen. They both climb up the stairs to our counting-room daily, call our big clock a "time destroyer" and so vie with each other in their efforts to handle the truth carelessly that it is often a question who comes off victor in these verbal contests. However, the skipper with the false ivories generally fails to get the last word, for he often loses his suction power by fast talking, and has to leave off to prevent his teeth from slipping down his œsophagus. Once again the air in the office assumes a nautical aroma, and we shall be well employed and well talked to death. A whole parcel of American ships are now about due, and the Bay will liven up again with the Stars and Stripes as it did some two months ago.

It rains every afternoon now, at about a quarter past three, and just after tiffin is over we begin to look for the thunder-clouds that predict the coming shower. The other day a huge waterspout formed out in the Bay, swirled along, gyrated about, scooted squarely through the shipping, and broke on the beach between our house and the Luneta. The cloud effects were extremely curious, and the whole display was a number not generally down on the day's programme.

The company who are putting in the new electric

lights seem to be doing good work, and it is expected that everything will be running by the end of the year. So far, Manila has been favored only with the dull light given by petroleum, previously brought out from New York, or over from China, and, curiously enough, the empty tins in which the oil has come seem to be almost as valuable as their contents. They are used here for about everything under the sun, the natives cover their roofs with tin from these sources, and some of those more musically inclined even make a petroleum can up into a trombone or cornet.

Our house by the sea continues to prove very pleasant, and, peculiarly enough, the surf seems to beat on the beach with the same sound that it has on the New England coast. The southwest breeze blows strong from the Bay each afternoon, and the cumulus clouds are becoming heavier and more numerous day by day. The artillery-band still favors us with music at the Luneta, but before long it looks as if the rains would interrupt the afternoon promenade.

The black plague at Hong Kong does not seem to diminish, as was expected, and it is said that many people are leaving the city. All steamers coming from that port to this suffer a fortnight's quarantine down the Bay, and, if the difficulty continues much longer, Manila markets will be destitute of two of their chief staples—mutton and potatoes—both of which have to come across from China, or down from Japan. And speaking of sheep, Captain Tayler, of the Esmeralda, has had another of his usual interesting experiences with the custom-house. Just as his vessel, fresh from quarantine and Hong Kong, had been visited by the doctor, on her way to her berth some distance up the river, one of the sheep died. Rule number something-or-other in the Code of the Sanidad says that anything or anybody dying during the day must be buried before sundown, under penalty, for neglect, of $50. Rule number something-else in the Customs Code, however, says that the captain of any vessel turning out cargo short or in excess of the amount called for by the manifest shall be fined $100 for each piece too many or too little. If my good friend, the Captain, buried the sheep, he would be fined $100 at the custom-house for short out-turn. If he didn't bury it, the Board of Health would come down on him for $50, for neglecting regulations. The Captain, being a wise man, decided that it was more politic to be in the right with the doctor than with the officials at the custom-house, and at some considerable expense sent the sheep on shore and had it buried with due honors. He could not have thrown it into the river, for this would have been to incur an additional fine. Next morning, he presented the ship's manifest and a sheep's tail at the custom-house and the discharge of the live stock was begun. But, tail or no tail, the officials found the ship one sheep short and the Esmeralda was fined $100. Not quite so barefaced as the swindling of the poor skipper who came over from China with a load of paving-stones for Manila's Street Department. His vessel turned out seven paving-stones too many, and the fine was $700.

In the language of Daniel Webster, I " refrain from saying" that a few dollars or a good dinner, bestowed upon the right person, in Manila, often go a long way toward throwing some official off the scent in his hungry search for irregularity, but am willing to admit that, in dealing with customs men who frequently "examine" cases of champagne by drinking up the contents of a bottle from each one in order to see that the liquid is not chloroform or cologne, one must keep his purse full, his talk cool, and his temper on ice.

June 25, 1894.

Last Monday was the monthly bank-holiday again, and three of us had previously decided to take a journey southward for the purpose of seeing one of Luzon's active volcanoes and getting a little change of air and "chow."

So, late on Saturday afternoon, we went aboard a

dirty little steamer, which was to take us ninety miles down the coast. She wasn't as big as a good-sized tug and was laden with multicolored natives, who were on their way back to the provinces after a brief shopping expedition to the capital. We were soon sailing out past the fleet of larger vessels in the Bay, with our dull prow pointed to the mouth of the great inclosed body of water. At nightfall we reached the Corregidor light-house, at the Bay's entrance, and thence our course lay to the south. At half-past two that night our craft reached a place called Taal. During our trip down we had become acquainted with a very pleasant Indian sugar-planter, who is as well off in dollars as rich in hospitality. At Taal he took us to one of the three big houses he owns, and, although only three o'clock in the morning, gave us a delicious breakfast. We talked and chatted away comfortably, and as the first streaks of dawn appeared I played several appropriate selections on one of the two very good-toned pianos belonging to his establishment. This brought out his family, and before we set out for the river from which our start to the volcano was to be made, quite a social gathering was in progress.

The natives all through the islands seemed indeed most courteous and hospitable to foreigners, and although a Spaniard hesitates to show his face outside of any of the garrison towns, yet any of the other European bipeds is known in a minute and well treated. Our good friend at Taal went so far as to harness up a pair of ponies and drive us down to the river at four o'clock in the morning, and we found a large *banca*, previously ordered, waiting to take us up to the Lake of Taal and across to the volcano.

Our *banca* was of good size, was rowed by seven men and steered by one, and had a little thatched hen-coop arrangement over the stern, to keep the sun off our heads. We had brought one "boy" with us from Manila, with enough "chow" to last for two days, and soon all was stowed away in our floating tree-trunk. The river was shallow, and for most of the six miles of its length poles were the motive-power. It was slow work, and both wind and current were hostile. In due course, however, the lake came into view, and in its centre rose the volcano, smoking away like a true Filipino. The wind was now blowing strong and unfavorable, and we saw that it was not going to be an easy row across the six or seven miles of open water to the centre island. But the men worked with a will, and although the choppy waves slopped over into our roost once or twice so jocosely that it almost seemed as if we should have to turn back, we kept on. Benefitting by a lull or two, our progress was gradual, and at half after twelve, seven hours from Taal, we landed on the volcanic island and prepared for an ascent.

The lake of Taal is from fifteen to twenty miles across, is surrounded by high hills and mountains, for the most part, and has for its centre the volcanic island upon whose edges rise the sloping sides of an active cone a thousand feet high. The lake is certainly good to look at, reminding one forcibly of Loch Lomond, and the waters, shores, and mountains around all seem to bend their admiring gaze on the little volcano in its centre.

Filling our water-jug, we set off up the barren lava-slopes of this nature's safety-valve, sweltering under the stiff climb in the hot sun. Happily, the view bettered each moment, the smell of the sulphur became stronger, and we forgot present discomfort in anticipations of the revelation to come. After banging our shins on the particularly rough lava-beds of the ascent, near the top, we saw a great steaming crater yawning below us and sending up clouds of sulphurous steam. In the centre of this vast, dreary Circus Maximus rose a flat cone of red-hot squashy material, and out of it ascended the steam and smoke. All colors of the rainbow played with each other in the sun, and farther to the right was a boiling lake of fiery material that was variegated enough to suit an Italian organ-grinder.

It was all very weird, and if we had not been so lazy we should probably have descended farther into this laboratory of fire than we did. But it was too hot to make matches of ourselves and the air smelt like the river Styx at low tide. So we were contented with a good view of the wonders of the volcano from a distance, enjoyed the panorama from the narrow encircling apex-ridge, and cooled off in the smart breeze. Once more at the lake, and it was not long before we were in it, tickling our feet on the rough cinders of the bottom. The bath was most rejuvenating after a hot midday climb, and just to sit in the warmish water up to one's neck gave one a sort of mellow feeling like that presumably possessed by a ripe apple ready to fall on the grass.

The wind was now fresher than ever and more unfavorable to our course. The captain of the tree-trunk, in a tone quite as authoritative as that manipulated by the commander of an ocean liner, said we could not proceed for some time, so the boy arranged the provisions and we had a meal in our little hencoop. After a provoking wait until four o'clock the old *banca* was pushed off again and the struggle renewed. The seven men, who had now been poling and rowing since early morning, seemed pretty well beat, but there was no shelter on the volcanic islands

Puentes de Ayala, which Help two of Manila's Suburbs to Shake Hands Across the Pasig.

and we had to push on. The other shore looked far away and we slopped forward sluggishly. The sun set, the moon rose, and still we were buffeting with the choppy waves. It reminded me a good deal of the sea of Galilee; and it did seem as if the dickens himself was blowing at us and trying to keep us from ever getting to that farther shore.

At last we reached the lee of a lofty perpendicular island part way across the lake, and, although its upright sides offered no chance to land, yet they kept off that southeast wind. The men shut their teeth hard, and in due course moved our bark around the point and out into more moonlight and breeze. The lights and shadows on the great lump of rock standing a thousand feet out of the water behind us were worth looking at, and in many places huge basaltic columns seemed to be holding up the mass above. Not to put as much labor into these lines as our men put into the oars, at half after ten we came to land, seven hours from the shore of the volcano, a distance which in fair wind ought to be covered in a little over one.

On shore there seemed to be about four huts, two pig-sties, and nothing more. Stared at by a crowd of natives whom our arrival suddenly incubated from somewhere, and who swarmed down to see who we were, we talked with our boatman, but only succeeded in finding out that we had come to a place not down on the map or on the highroad to the next village whither we were bound. It was simply a collection of huts, children, and pigs, situated at the lake's edge and connected with the outer world by a foot-path that led up over the hills eight miles to the nearest pueblo. To walk those eight miles at eleven o'clock was out of the question, and to sleep in one of those little dirty huts ashore was just as bad. The crowd of natives had grown, and so, to avoid being over-run with the eminently curious, we pushed off from shore and anchored out in the lake, to eat a little "chow" and decide what to do. Weariness tempered our decision, which was to sleep where we were, in the *banca*, under the hen-coop, and, having made it known to our trusty but hard-looking crew, they fell down like shots and, in less than a minute, were asleep in all sorts of jackstraw positions. One slept on the oars, another on the poles, a third on our collection of volcanic rocks, a fourth in the bottom of the boat, a fifth sitting up, and a sixth—I don't know where.

We three lay down side by side in the little cooped-over roost, and found there was just room to reside like sardines in a box. Our feet were out under the stars at one side, our heads at the other, and there we were, and there we slept, in an unknown wilderness.

Though no one could change his position we all rested fairly well, and nothing happened to mar the beauty of the night. As the sun reddened the east, feeling more like awakened chickens than anything else, we packed up, paid out some of the heavy dollars, that made each of us feel like sinkers on a fish-line, and loaded what little luggage we had upon a bony pony ashore. Adieus were said to the lake and to our crew, and our little caravan started up a broad foot-path for the village of Tanauan, about eight miles away. It was a long walk, on no refreshment save a night's sleep in a hen-coop, but after passing over hills and dales, by *nipa* huts of all sizes and descriptions, and after being stared at by curious natives, we arrived at our destination, a good-sized village, in two and a half hours. We responded to an invitation of the captain of the pueblo, to take possession of his house, and got up a very decent breakfast out of our fast depleting stock. The old captain treated us most cordially, and after a three-hours' stay helped us to load ourselves and our chattels aboard two stout-wheeled, *carromatas* each hitched to two ponies.

Off again, once more, our course was shaped overland toward the other great lake up back of Manila, by which the return was to be made. The road was fearful, the ruts two feet deep in places, and the bad sections far more numerous than the good pieces.

We got stuck in the mud, had to pry our conveyances and the ponies out, and I fear did not enjoy the beauties of the rather tame scenery on the way. At last the crest of a hill brought the *Laguna de Bay* in sight, and in less than an hour we reached the village of Calamba, on its shores. A shabby little native house was put at our disposal after we boldly walked up and took possession of it; a swarm of children were shoved out of the one decent room, and in a short time our boy was giving us canned turtle-soup and herrings. In the afternoon we merely lounged about the town and took a swim in the lake, while in the evening, early after the very good little dinner gotten up by our servant there was nothing to do but to turn in, even though the house was surrounded by the curious, who had looked in at the windows to watch people dining with knives, forks, plates, and napkins.

The floor of our room was of bamboo slats, just below whose many openings were four fighting-cocks and when bed-time came we were tired enough to tumble down on the canes just as we stood. The cock who sang out of tune woke us at about sunrise Tuesday morning, and after one more swim in the lake we packed up our traps and prepared ourselves to take the little Manila steamer that left at eight o'clock on its thirty-mile return trip. The sail down the lake and into the Pasig River was cool, delightful, and without incident, and at noon Tuesday we pulled up at the wharf at Manila, having completed an almost perfect circle of travel one hundred and fifty miles in circumference, to be heartily congratulated on having successfully made a trip which few perform but many covet. My own cane sleeping machine seemed good again after hen-coops and bamboo floors, and smooth roads and civilization far better than ruts and rickety *carromatas*.

VI

First Storm of the Rainy Season—Fourth of July—Chinese "Chow" Dogs—Crullers and Pie and a Chinese Cook—A Red-Letter Day—The China-Japan War—Manila Newspapers—General Blanco and the Archbishop—An American Fire-Engine and its Lively Trial—The Coming of the Typhoon—Violence of the Wind—The Floods Next—Manila Monotony.

July 4th.

THE mails have been badly snarled up lately, and although nobody has received any letters for nearly two weeks, none are expected for about ten days. The other morning began the first real storm of the rainy season, and we came very near having a bad typhoon, but someone turned the switch, and it swirled up the back coast on the Pacific side and crossed through a notch in the mountains, some distance to the north of Manila, giving the city only four days of monstrous winds and floods of rain. The streets were two feet deep with water in the business section, and down at our house by the sea the wind blew so hard that it carried the tin from our roof off to visit the next suburb. Then it was that those sturdy windows of small sea-shells set into hardwood lattice seemed far more secure than glass, and I doubt if anything less well constructed would have stood the blast that surged in from the broad bay.

Going down-town in the morning, my carriage was slid clean across the road by the force of the wind, and once it seemed as if I might be lifted up into the low clouds that scudded close to the tops of the bamboo-trees. Huge seas came tumbling ashore on the beach, and the vessels in the great exposed Bay had all they could do to hang to their anchors, as the surf sometimes dashed as high as their lower foreyards.

The natives never carry umbrellas in the rain, but march along and do not seem to mind getting wet to the skin. They do indeed look bedraggled in their thin clothes, that cling like sticking-plaster, and it seems as if they would get the fever. During the present blow, the single pony hitched to a tram-car often found his load moving him astern, and it was only by leaving the whole car wide open, so that the air could have free passage through from end to end and side to side, that he now and then made headway against the blast. This was not pleasant for the passengers, but made less demand on the motive-power. The bands at the Luneta have played when they got a chance, but the wind howls in from the Bay, as a rule, louder than the tunes bowl out of their brass instruments.

To-day seems to be the Glorious Fourth, and my colleague and I have just come back from the shipping, where the Captain of the Helen Brewer asked us to eat a celebrative dinner. All the ships in the Bay were dressed with flags, and the Brewer, which possessed more than her share, had a long line stretched from the bowsprit over the three masts down to the stern. Everybody was interested in the feast, and the Captain with the false teeth, who comes from New Hampshire, sent over a goose and some mince-pies. Eight of us sat down in the cozy saloon and partook of a meal altogether too hearty for the climate. The day was cool and overcast, and we spent a lazy afternoon on deck, listening to yarns told by two old salts who seemed to have had more than their share of wrecks, typhoons, and other adventures.

When we came ashore, at about sunset, there was gathered up from the remains of the feast the "seven basketsful," and we each went back in the launch, decorated with a bag of doughnuts under one arm and a bag of mince-pies under the other.

One of our small family of dogs was run over by the tram-car the other morning, in front of the house, and now rests in peace in a little grave down on the beach, hard by the rhythmic cadence of the waves. His little brother, who was suffering at the time from the

Calzada de San Sebastian. Iron Church in the Background "Made in Germany" and Brought Out in Pieces.

distemper, was so grieved at the loss that he too speedily faded away, and now lies close beside the other victim of circumstances. On the tombstone is a touching epitaph:

> "Pompey and Nettie, here they lie;
> Born to live, they had to die.
> The wheels of fate ran over one,
> The other was by grief undone."

Most of the large army of dogs that make a Manila night hideous are of that mongrel order, which is always looking for something to eat, but now and then one sees a good many of the so-called Chinese "chow"-dogs about the streets, and with their black tongues, long hair, and peculiar bushy tails that curl sharply up over their backs, they are quite as interesting, as unaffectionate. Over in China they make very good eating up to the age of three months, and from this fact derive the "chow" part of their name. Although they are very susceptible to changes of locality and climate, we are now making negotiations to have one brought over to take the place of the dear departed eulogized above. And later, I may even try the experiment of having one for Sunday dinner—if he doesn't make a good pet.

The doughnuts which I brought home from the Brewer have proved very interesting to my cook, and I have been obliged to count them each day for purposes of security. He now watches me closely as I make away with one or two for breakfast, to see just what effect these marvellous looking "fried holes" have on my intellect. I notice he looks to see if there are any crumbs left, from which he might gather an inkling as to the composition of these curios; but so far there haven't been any crumbs. As he is cooking for us now, instead of the Chinese gentleman that we originally had, this curiosity is but natural, and some day he will probably try to furnish us with the native-made article. In fact he has already tried the experiment of concocting a mince-pie after the general appearance of one of the earlier donations made by a captain in the Bay, and the result was worthy of description. As I arranged to measure the original pie after each meal, before locking it up in our safe, in order to protect it from disappearing, my faithful cook could only guess as to its composition by sundry glances from afar. But being of an inventive mind he conceived the idea of chopping up some well-done roast beef, mixing with it some sugar and raisins, roofing it over with a thatch of pastry, and serving it for dessert. And then as we came to the course in question he stood in the doorway waiting for our verdict. His effort was worthy of all praise, but his pie was damnable, and pieces of it went sailing out the windows.

July 28th.

On the 20th instant a steamer arrived from Hong Kong, and had the honor of being the first vessel to come in from that port in thirty days. She was supposed to have three American mails aboard, but it turned out that they were down to arrive by the vessel coming in six days later. I came to the office the other morning, and looking toward my desk, found it almost invisible. It looked as if somebody in the neighborhood were the editor of a paper, and as if all the spring poets in the universe had sent their manuscripts for inspection. The desk groaned beneath the bulky chaos of three mails from the United States, delayed in transmission by the black plague, and fumigated together down the bay. But no sooner had we gotten through the first course of an epistolary feast than the captain of a large four-masted ship shuffled into the room and deposited a huge pot of steaming baked beans, just fresh from his steward's galley-stove, on the table. What with beans, letters, magazines, and comic papers, it might be said our day was a red-letter one.

The other day my colleague and I took dinner off aboard the Nagato Maru, a smart steamer just in from Japan, and captained by an American who knows what it is to set a good table. It seems that the China-Japan war has actually broken out in all its glory, and as there is a vague rumor that a Chinese war-ship is waiting outside to capture this very same steamer, she is going to stay here for awhile.

The Japanese have sunk several Chinese transport ships already, and one of the unfortunate craft used to come here to Manila. In other directions the Chinese are said to have beaten the Japs badly on land, but over in this slow old moth-eaten place the daily papers will publish cablegrams from Spain by the page, that give out nothing but official stuff and Government appointments; and when it comes to something of real interest, like a war, they will either be without any news whatever, or tell the whole story wrong side out in a single line, that may or may not be true. And so you are probably getting better news of this whole affair, twelve thousand miles away, than we are, who are almost on the field of action.

Our Manila papers consist of four pages, the first two of which are especially reserved for advertisements. Half of one of the inside leaves is likewise reserved, and the remaining half is covered with blocks full of gloomy sentiments which relate to the decease of this or that person. There is a little black frame of type around each square, and at the top is a cross, with a "R. I. P." or "D. O. M." under it. Below comes the name of the defunct, with hour, minute, day, and year of his birth and death, and below his virtues are extolled and his friends invited to pray for the repose of his soul. Every year, each person that has died the year before has his anniversary, both in church and in the newspapers; and when you recollect that out of a population of 350,000 a good many depart each twelvemonth, it is hard to see why the whole paper shouldn't consist of these notices. The other inside page contains the news, and we learn that a bad odor has been discovered up some side-street; that a dog fell into the river and was drowned; that a perfumery store has received a new kind of liquefied scent; that it will probably rain in some part of the island during the day; and that the band on the Luneta ought not to be frightened off merely by a few drops that fall from some passing cloud. And so it goes until the French or English mail comes in, and then the progressive dailies copy all the news they can find, out of the foreign papers, and serve it up cold, æt. one month.

I met General Blanco, Governor of the islands, the other evening, and he seemed to enjoy the good music and good supper which one of our popular bank-managers and his wife provided for some of us in the colony on the occasion of a birthday. He is an elderly man, and kindly, and appears milder in disposition than would seem advisable for one occupying so important a position. I should think he might let some of those sharp-eyed little ministers of his run him, and he appears almost too modest, too kind-hearted, to be the ruler that he is. Suffice to say the General is modest in dress and modest in manner. He often walks up and down the Malecon promenade by the Bay in the afternoon, saluting everyone that passes, and when the vesper bells ring out the hour of prayer from one of the old churches inside the city walls he stops, removes his tall gray stove-pipe and, as do a host of other pedestrians, bows his head. To tell the truth he has little of the Spanish aspect about him and is just the kind of a man one would go up and speak to on the Teutonic or Campania. In sharp contrast is he to the Archbishop, who drives about behind his fine white horses and looks as keen as well-nourished. But who knows! Appearances are deceitful, and foolish he who trusts to them.

August 11th.

Two steamers have just come in from Hong Kong and are tied up in quarantine down at Marivelis, at the mouth of the Bay. The mail ought to be here in forty-eight hours, but two days is a very short time to give Manila postal authorities, for they really are slow enough to desire four—one in which to make up their minds to send a launch, two in which to go, three in which to come back, and four in which to distribute the results of their camphorated fumigation.

The most noteworthy thing that has happened in the way of excitement since the last mail was the operating of the new American fire-engine, which we imported from the States for the wealthy proprietor of our hemp-press, who is part Spaniard, part native, and part Chinese. It seems he was up in our office one day, and on the centre-table saw a catalogue containing pictures of a collection of our modern fire-fighters. He asked what those things were, and, on being told that they were used to put out fires, said he wanted one at once, the biggest we could get him, in order that he might reduce the insurance he was paying on his large store-houses and still go on collecting the premiums from those whose goods were in his charge.

Although ours is an exporting business, and we do not know much about fire-engines, yet the occasion seemed auspicious, the prospect of payment sure, and the outlook interesting. The result was that we forwarded the order to New York by the first mail, and the other day, after four months of waiting, the pieces of the big engine came over on the Esmeralda, in big cases. They were very heavy, and the natives began the exhibition by nearly dropping the boiler into the river as they attempted to hoist it into a lighter. To skip over the difficulties which were encountered in hoisting the cases onto the quay in front of the offices of our well-to-do purchaser, we come to the mental hardships that were encountered in putting the machine together; for no one in Manila had ever seen a Yankee fire-engine before, and although we had a full description of the complicated mechanism, with drawings of the parts, and numbers where each piece was to fit onto some other piece, there was no one in town who could help us much in getting it into working order.

Fortunately, the hemp business was dull and my colleague and I were thus enabled to give more attention to this Chinese puzzle than if the fibre market had been booming. The red wheels with gold stripes were the first thing to be adjusted, and the eyes of the onlookers who happened to be strolling up and down the quay opened to large dimensions as the covering was stripped from the nickel-plated boiler and the process of establishment went on. At last the big machine was on its feet, with valves and gear adjusted, and with the slight assistance which we got from a Spanish engineer who knew something about marine machinery, we found out that the whistle ought not to be screwed onto the safety-valve.

Several Englishmen who happened to come by in the early stages of our efforts made sarcastic com-

Ploughing in the Rice-fields with the Carabao.

A copy of which was sent to an American concern, who thought there was business for steam-ploughs in the Philippines. They don't think so now.

ments on the appearance of our new toy, and could not see how an affair with so much gold paint on the wheels and so much nickel on the boiler was going to work successfully. But we did not say much, since we were well occupied in trying to find out the proper way to fill the boiler. Someone suggested pouring the water down the whistle, and so, mounted on a step-ladder, one to us began the interesting experiment. The water seemed to run in all right, as it gurgled down through the pipes, and did not leak out of the bottom. As there did not seem to be any other loophole to the boiler, we concluded this must be the right method, and took turns for an hour in emptying the contents of an old kerosene tin into the whistle-valve.

Next, with great trepidation, we started a fire in the grate, and were rejoiced to see that the new engine was soon fuming away like an old veteran. It quite spruced us up to hear the fire crackle under the boiler; but our heads became even more swelled when steam enough was generated to tickle the feed-pump into taking care of all the vacant lots in the boiler-tubes.

When our friend Don Capitan found that the engine was going to work and knew its business, he said we must have a big trial and let all Manila see the show. To this end he sent around printed programmes of what was going to take place, to all the prominent people in the city—for he was an Alderman, by the way—inviting them to inspect the working of the engine and partake of a collation afterward in the spacious buildings of the hemp-press.

Wednesday, the fatal day, arrived, and the great American fire-engine stood out on the quay glistening in the sun, the centre of an admiring crowd of open-mouthed natives. The Englishmen in the background rather put their heads together and shook them the wrong way, as they often do at anything American, but the natives allowed their lower lips to drop from overwhelming admiration. Everybody was curious, and all were expectant, from the small kids dressed in nothing but the regulation Philippine undershirt, who played shinney with the coal for the boiler and looked down the hose-nozzle, to Don Capitan himself, who went around shaking by the hands all the high and mighty officials who had come to see his latest freak. My associate and I felt fairly important as we gruffly ordered the police to clear the ground for action and blew the whistle to scare the audience. The huge suction-hose was run into the river, and our host made his pet servant jump in after it to hold the strainer out of the mud. Ten natives were stationed at the nozzle of the four-inch hose, which was pointed up the small plaza running back from the quay, and while I poked up the fire to give us a little impressive smoke, Rand rang the bell and turned on steam.

The affair worked admirably, and the big stream of yellow water went so far as to gently soak down a lot of baled tobacco that was lying on a street-corner at the next block, supposedly beyond reach. The owner of the tobacco, thinking that a thunder-storm had struck the town, came to the door of his office, just behind, to see what was up, and, as the engine suddenly began to work a little better, the stream of water somehow knocked him over and played around the entrance to his storehouse. At the rate things were going it looked as if the exhibition would prove expensive and, to avoid diplomatic complications, we shut off steam long enough to shift the hose over for a more unobstructed spurt along the river.

In a few moments after the change had been made an open throttle made a truly huge torrent belch from the long nozzle with such force as to make the ten hose-men feel decidedly nervous, but it did not stop them from turning the stream toward a lighter which was being polled down the Pasig by two Malays. The foremost was washed backward into the lighter, and the hindmost swept off into the river as if he had been a cockroach. A Chinaman who was paddling a load of vegetables to the Esmeralda in a hollow tree-trunk suffered the same fate. He and his greens were swished out of the *banca* in an instant, and he found himself sitting on his inverted craft floating helplessly down-stream.

Then suddenly, as we opened the throttle to the last notch, the hose-men, in their excitement to wet some coolies loading hemp, far up the quay, tried to turn the torrent back onto the pavement, but, with its force of fifteen hundred gallons to the minute, it was too quick for them, and with one mighty "kerchug" broke away to send the nozzle flying around like a mill-wheel. Before they knew what struck them the ten men holding the nozzle were knocked prostrate, and two small boys in undershirts, who were playing around in the mud-puddles near by, were whisked off into the river like so much dust. A dozen lightning wriggles of the hose, and the frenzied cataract shot a third boy through the wire door into the office of our friend, Don Capitan. Inside the door, on a wooden settee, were sitting some of the family servants holding their infants, and the same stream on which the boy travelled through the door washed the whole party, settee and all, across the hallway into a heap at the foot of the stairs.

Outside, the audience stampeded, and the man in

the river, holding on to the suction hose, had hard work to prevent being drawn up through the strainer and pumped out the other end in fragments. All this took place in a quarter of the time it takes to tell of it, and events followed each other in such quick succession that the hose had started to turn over on its back and charge on the engine before one of us rushed in to shut off steam. The two boys washed into the river were fished out more dead than alive, but more frightened than hurt, and the native Philippine policeman on duty at the front arrested them promptly for daring to be drowned. The boy blown through the screen-door had his ear badly torn, and was likewise arrested for not entering the house in a more civilized manner. The natives nursed their bare feet stepped on in the rush; the Englishmen, who had been sarcastic several days before, said nothing; but the Spaniards asked where the collation was, and, waterlogged though they were, began to eat like good ones. The policeman marched the three boys in undershirts to the station-house, and next morning the daily newspapers devoted more space than was usual in describing the wonderful machinery that came from America, for the benefit of their readers, who, like that English dude of old, " didn't weahlly dweam that so much wattah could come out of such a wehwey diminootive-looking affaiah."

Otherwise, in Manila we are now enjoying the so-called *veranillo*, or little summer, which every year comes along about the middle of August, and which consists of two or three weeks of cool, pleasant weather, that comes between the rains of July and the typhoon season of September. And fine weather it is, with a jolly breeze blowing in from the China Sea all day, with delightful afternoons, moonlight nights, and fresh mornings.

September 20th.

There has been no opportunity to start letters off for the other side of the globe since the early days of the present month, on account of a typhoon which has visited our fair capital, and which has so delayed steamers that all connections seem to have been scattered to the four winds. I have long been waiting to become acquainted with one of these aërial disturbances, and at last the meteorological monotony has been broken.

Early in this eventful week, warnings came from our most excellent observatory, run by the Jesuit priests, that trouble was brewing down in the Pacific to the south and east, and by Friday signal No. 1 of the danger system was displayed on the flagstaff of the look-out tower. The news about the storm was indefinite, but the villain was supposed to be slowly moving northwest, headed directly for Manila. Saturday up went signal No. 2, and in the afternoon No. 3, and by evening No. 4. Still everything was calm and peaceful, and Sunday morning dawned pleasant but for the exception of a dull haze. Early in the afternoon up went signal No. 5, which means that things are getting pretty bad, and which is not far from No. 8, the worst that can be hoisted.

Everybody now began to get ready for the invisible monster. All the steamers and ships in the river put out extra cables, and the vessels in the Bay extra anchors. No small craft of any kind were permitted to pass out by the breakwater, and later navigation in the river itself was prohibited. Still everything was calm and quiet, but the haze thickened and low scud-clouds began to sail in from the China Sea. Shortly after tiffin at our residence by the seaside, our gaze was attracted by a native coming down the street, dressed in a black coat with shirt-tails hanging out beneath, and wearing white trousers and a tall hat. He carried a decorated cane, wore no shoes, and marched down the centre of the street, giving utterance to solemn sentences in a deep musical voice. In short, he was the official crier to herald the coming of the typhoon, and as he marched along the bells up in the old church beyond our house rang out what poets would call "a wild, warning plea."

The natives opposite began hastily to sling ropes over the thatch of their light shanties, and one of the Englishmen who lived not far back of us had already stretched good solid cables over the steep-sloping roof of his domicile. A sort of hush prevailed, and then sudden gusts began to blow in off the bay. The scud-clouds increased and appeared to be in a fearful hurry. The roar of the surf loudened, and one after the other of our sliding sea-shell windows had to be shut and bolstered up for precaution. The typhoon seemed to be advancing slowly, as they often do, but its course was sure. Our eight o'clock dinner-hour passed and the wind began to howl. Before turning in for the night, we moved out of our little parlor such valuable articles as might be most missed if they decided to journey off through the air in company with the roof, and later tried to sleep amidst a terrific din of rattlings. But slumber was impossible. Our house trembled like a blushing bride before the altar, and for the triumphal music of the "Wedding March" the tin was suddenly stripped off our rain-shed roof like so much paper. And then the racket! Great pieces of tin were slapping around against the house like all possessed; the trees in the front garden were sawing against the cornices, as if they wanted to get in, and the rush of air outside seemed to generate a vacuum within.

Types of True Filipinos Waiting to Call Themselves Americans.

At 3 A.M. things got so bad that it seemed as if something were going to burst, and my chum and I decided to take a last look into the parlor before seeking the safety of the cellar. No glass would have withstood the gusts that came pouncing in from the Bay, but our sea-shell windows did not seem to yield. The rain was sizzling in through the cracks like hot grease when a fresh doughnut is dropped into the spider, and the noise outside was deafening. As our house seemed to be holding together, however, we gave up going to the regions below, and turned in again, thankful that we were not off on the ships in the Bay. Now and then the wind lulled somewhat, and blew from another quarter, but by early morning came some of the most terrific blowings I have ever felt, resulting from the change of direction. Down came all the wires in the main street; over went half a dozen *nipa* houses to one side of us, and "kerplunk" broke off some venerable trees that for many years had withstood the blast. The street was a mass of wreckage, as far down as the eye could see, and few signs of life were visible. During the rest of the day the wind blew most fiercely, but from the change of direction it was easy to see that the centre of the typhoon was passing off to the northwest.

I sallied out later in the afternoon, dressed in not much more than a squash-hat, a rubber coat, and a pair

of boots, whose soles were holy enough to let the water
out as fast as it came in. It was as much as one
could do to stand against the blast, but I managed
to keep along behind the houses, cross the streets,
and reach the Luneta, where all the lamps bent their
heads with broken glass, and where the huge waves
were flying far up into the air in their efforts to dispose of the stone sea-wall. The clumps of fishing
and bath houses which stood perched on posts
out in the surf were being fast battered to pieces,
and those which were not minus roof and sides were
washed up into the road as driftwood. The natives
were rushing gingerly hither and thither, grabbing
such logs as they could find, while some of the fishermen's families were crouching behind a stone wall
watching their wrecked barns, and sitting on their
saucepans, furniture, and babies, to keep them from
sailing skyward. The surf was tremendous, the
vessels in the bay were shrouded in spray, and several
of them seemed almost to be ashore in the breakers.
A steamer appeared to have broken adrift and was
locked in the embrace of a Nova Scotia bark. But
everything comes to an end and as night drew on
the winds and rain subsided and comparative quiet
succeeded a season of exaggerated movement and
din.

The typhoon was wide in diameter, perhaps two

hundred miles, and so was not destructive, like the one that laid Manila low way back in the '80's. It seems that the larger the diameter of one of these circular storms, the less its intensity, and although the wind at any given time is moving with tremendous velocity within the circle, the whole disturbance is not advancing at a pace much over a dozen miles an hour.

After the typhoon came the floods, and the old Pasig covered the adjacent country. The water concealed the road to the up-town club at Nagtajan under a depth of several feet, and one could without difficulty row into the billiard-room or play water-polo in the bowling-alley. Two of my friends were nearly drowned by trying to drive when they should have swum or gone by boat. The pony walked off with their carriage into a rice-field, in the darkness, and was drowned in more than eight feet of water. The boys only crawled out with difficulty, and just managed to reach "dry land" (that with three feet of water over it) in the nick of time. As it was, one of them practically saved the other's life, and has since been presented with a gold watch, which does not run.

One of the bank-managers was to give a dinner-dance at his house next evening, to which everyone was invited, when word came that his bungalow could only be reached by boats, and that the festivities would have to be put off until the parlor floor appeared. To the north, where the actual centre of the typhoon passed, the railway was swept away, the telegraph line that connects with the cable to Hong Kong torn down, and the country in general laid under water. But the show is now concluded, and business, which had been paralyzed for a week, once more starts up with the coming of the cablegrams.

Manila life goes on as ever, and it is curious to note how fast the days and weeks slip backward. Everyone agrees that the most rapid thing in town, except the winds of the typhoons, is the speed with which the Philippine to-day becomes yesterday. The secret seems to lie in the fact that there are no landmarks by which to remember the weeks that are gone. The trees are green all the year round, and there are no snow-storms to mark the contrast between winter and summer. There are no class-days, no ball-games, and no coming out in spring fashions to break the orderly procession of the sun, moon, and stars. We wear our white starched suits every day in the year, and one's wardrobe is not replete with various checks, plaids, and stripes that mark an epoch in one's appearance. We cannot, like *Teufelsdröch*, in "Sartor Resartus," speculate much on the "clothes philosophy," though we may do so on the centres of indifference; for our garments are not complex enough to invite transcendental theorizing. Manila food is alike from Christmas morn to the following Christmas eve, and so, take it all in all, the past is practically without milestones, and seems far shorter than one in which many events make the measured steps more clearly differentiated.

At present everybody dates his ideas from the typhoon, and that will remain a landmark for some time, if the fire which took place the other evening on the banks of the river does not usurp its position. Ten thousand bales of hemp, and a lot of copra, sugar, and cocoanut-oil were sent aloft in less earthly form. Æsthetically the sight was beautiful, and the eye was charmed by the mingling of vast tongues of blue, green, red, and yellow flames, some of which burst forth from the very waters of the river itself on which the inflammable materials had excursioned. Our new fire-engine was on hand for the first time, in actual service, and, together with the small English engine brought out from London, did its duty. America, as usual, was in the lead, and everybody stood aghast to see the big five-inch stream mow down the brick walls of the burning houses like grain before the reaper. One native in particular, whose frail hut was washed to splinters by that big cataract played upon it to save it from the flames, said he'd rather lose his property by fire than to stand by and see the blooming *bomba* (fire-engine) blow it all to bits. The local department, as usual, lost their heads, and while some began to chop the tiles off the roofs of neighboring houses, others directed the streams from the hand-pumps onto the choppers. Even our gallant friend the American broker, who helps swell the number of Yankee business men in Manila to four, almost got roasted alive by being shut into an iron vault as he tried to rescue some valuable papers belonging to a customer and had to be soused with water, after his miraculous escape, to lower his temperature. But at length Providence and water prevailed, and the damage did not come to more than half a million dollars.

VII

A Series of Typhoons—A Chinese Feast-day—A Bank-holiday Excursion—Lost in the Mist—Los Banos—The "Enchanted Lake"—Six Dollars for a Human Life—A Religious Procession—Celebration of the Expulsion of the Chinese—Bicycle Races and Fireworks.

October 5th.

PHEW! We have hardly had time to breathe since the last mail, for we have been in the midst of typhoon after typhoon, shipwrecks, house-wrecks, and telegraph-wrecks, both simplex and duplex. Manila had scarcely gotten over talking of the war of the elements, above spoken of, before another cyclone was announced to the south, and soon we were going through an experience similar to that related the other day. When that was over, everybody began to draw breath again, but before the lungs of the populace were fully expanded, the wind suddenly went into that dangerous quarter, the northwest, and up went signal No. 5 again. The blow came on more suddenly than the former one, and all hands left the business offices to go home and sit on their roofs. The tin was again stripped like paper from our portico, and great masses of metal banged around outside with the clash of cymbals. It was a terrific night. The ships in the Bay dragged their anchors nearly to the breakwater, and in the morning four Spanish brigs were a total wreck. One in particular went ashore on the bar at the river's mouth, and at daylight was being swept fore and aft by the great seas. Eight men were hanging on for dear life, and it looked as if they would be swallowed up in the great drink; but two big lifeboats were got out, and as the sea moderated somewhat, the sailors were at length rescued, just as their ship went all to smash. A thousand houses were blown down, many of the streets in Manila were flooded, telegraph lines prostrated, and tram-car service interrupted.

But things have now quieted down, and Sunday was a big feast-day in the Chinese quarter. All the wealthy Chinamen were celebrating something or other, and they invited all the foreign merchants, as well as their local friends, to the celebration. They served tea and refreshments in their various little junk shops, and some of the more influential members of the colony of fifty thousand gave elaborate spreads, followed by dances and concerts. The streets were filled with peculiar processions of men carrying banners and graven images, and the sidewalks were lined with spectators.

I went to one of the most pretentious of the indoor

On the Banks of the Enchanted Lake. *See page* 141.

functions, found myself in a gorgeously furnished suite of apartments, decorated in true Chinese fashion, and was royally entertained by a shrewd Celestial who was supposed to be worth several million dollars. He began conversation with me by saying that, in his belief, bathing was injurious, and that he had not taken a bath in thirty years. From all I could judge, others of his brethren seemed to hold the same views as he, and the long rooms, halls, and corridors in due season got to be so warm and fragrant that it was a relief to escape.

Now and then the bells in the big church rang lustily, and many lanterns lighted it up from cornice to keystone. Hundreds of carriages drove through the streets, apparently bound nowhere in particular, and the bands played in all quarters.

It almost seems as if each week in the calendar brought in a religious display of some sort in some one part of the town, and every Sunday evening finds a big church somewhere blazing with light or a street blinking with candles.

November 13th.

The Monday after the departure of the monthly direct mail from Manila to the Peninsula is always devoted to our old friend "bank-holiday," and all the foreign merchants close their doors. This event occurred the first of this week, and on Saturday afternoon last some of the more energetic of us, deciding to take another little outing into the hills, started up the river on a small launch, bound for the big lake at the foot of the mountains. A drizzling rain was falling and the weather did not look propitious, but we pushed on, left the mouth of the river where the lake empties into it, and sallied out on the broad waters of the Laguna de Bay. Numerous serving-boys, boxes of china, food, ice, and bedding ballasted the stern of our little steamer, and as it grew dark a feast was prepared for us on deck. In going up the lake, the pilot, who was accustomed only to navigating the launch along the quays of Manila itself, got quite at sea and lost his way in the evening mist. Some of us, however, more nautical than the rest, procured a chart, consulted a compass which the native mariner in his stupidity chose utterly to disregard, and by dint of perseverance brought the frail bark back into her proper course, without further mishap than running through a series of fish-weirs.

We anchored near a little settlement, Los Baños, shortly before midnight. The deck planking did not make a soft bed, but nevertheless the snoring soon became hard likewise, and Sunday morning found us refreshed by the bracing air of the provinces. The rain had cleared away, and after an early breakfast the pilot ran the launch slowly ashore on a smooth beach, beneath a high bank fringed with bamboo. The gang-plank was run out, and several of our little party started off with guns to get some duck, snipe, and pigeons, which were plentiful in the jungle beyond.

Those of us who were left, with a couple of native guides, climbed up the steep slopes of an extinct volcano to explore a so-called "Enchanted Lake" that occupied the low crater. The way led past several ponds filled to overflowing with pink pond-lilies, and, as we wound up along the rising knolls, the air was as fragrant as that of a greenhouse. Then came a short climb which brought us to the crater's edge. The Enchanted Lake lay like a mirror below, and the rich foliage all about was almost perfectly reflected in the still, green water.

The locality being romantic, it is quite regular that there should be connected with it an interesting story which seems to bear on its face the evidences of truth. It seems there used to live a fisherman and his wife hard by the sloping banks that surround the Enchanted Lake. One day, so the story goes, the fisherman's spouse had reason to suspect the fidelity of her husband, and aflame with pious rage, she concocted a scheme to rid herself of her worser half. Calling upon two rival fishermen whose hut was not far distant, she promised them the large amount of twelve dollars if they would put her husband out of the way. This being a pot of money to them, they agreed to her proposition, and during one of the next excursions out to the distant fish-weirs in the parent lake below, contrived to tip him overboard and hold him under. Coming back in the afternoon, they went to the hut of the freshly made widow and demanded the twelve dollars.

"I can give you but six," said she, "for I'm hard up."

"But you promised us twelve if we would do the business," said they.

"But I tell you I can give you but six," responded the widow. "Take that or nothing."

Angry at having been thus deceived, the two murderers excitedly paddled over to the neighboring village of Los Baños, went to the *cuartel*, presided over by a Spanish official, and addressed him with these words:

"A lady over there by the Enchanted Lake promised us twelve dollars if we would kill her husband. We have done the job and asked her for our money, but she will only give us six. We want you to arrest her."

The official, thinking the whole thing a joke, laughingly said he would attend to the matter. The two simple-minded criminals went off, apparently satisfied, and disappeared.

Later, our friend the official thought there might be some truth behind the apparent absurdity of the yarn, and on investigation found that a murder had actually been committed. But someone more credulous than the Spaniard gave a friendly warning to the committers of the deed, and they were not brought to justice until some months afterward. Such is the comparative esteem in which the native holds human life and Mexican dollars.

Later we descended again to the bold coast-line of the Laguna de Bay and, to the accompaniment of banging guns, which showed that some of the rest of our party were really on the war-path, returned launch-ward. The hunting-expedition came in soon after with large bags of snipe and pigeon, and all hands then joined in a series of dives off the stern of our boat, or soused around in the tepid water. The group of savages living in the huts near by were much startled at our taking plunges headlong. They themselves never dive otherwise than feet first, for it is a common superstition among the Filipinos that the evil water-spirits would catch them by the head and hold them under if this article came along before the feet put in an appearance.

At noontime our native cooks did themselves proud in getting up a game breakfast, and in the afternoon the launch backed off and steamed across the narrow bay to Los Baños itself, a little town clustering around some boiling springs whose vapor floats over a good hotel and some elaborate bathing-establishments. This seems to be a rather favorite resort for the Spanish population of Manila at certain times of the year, and once or twice a week the old sidewheeler Laguna de Bay stops here on her way up from the capital to Santa Cruz.

Behind the town the land slopes steeply up to the mountain heights of still another extinct volcano, whose ghost exists merely to give life to the hot waters of the springs below. In front it runs off to the lake shore, and, all in all, the scenery is as picturesque as the air is healthy. From Los Baños we crossed the lake, cruised down along the abrupt mountainous shores between the two fine old promontories of Halla Halla, that jut out like the prongs to a W, and stopped every now and then at some particularly attractive little native village coming down to the water's edge. At about sundown on Monday afternoon, the prow was turned Manilaward, and after a cool sunset sail of twenty miles we drew in at the portico of the uptown club, all the better for our two day's trip, which cost us each but a little over five gold dollars.

Last night there occurred another one of those religious torchlight processions which are so common

In the Narrow Streets of Old Manila. A Procession. *See page* 145.

in the streets of Old Manila. It started after sunset, inside the city walls, from a big church brightly illuminated from top to bottom with small candle-cups that gave it the appearance of a great sugar palace. The procession consisted of many richly decorated floats, containing life-size figures of saints and apostles dressed in garments of gold and purple and borne along by sweating coolies, who staggered underneath a draping that shielded from view all save their lower limbs and naked feet. The larger floats were covered with dozens of candelabra and guarded by soldiers with fixed bayonets. Other rolling floats of smaller magnitude were pulled along by little children in white gowns, while troops of old maids, young maids, and Spanish women marched before and behind, dressed in black and carrying candles. The black mantillas which fell gracefully from the heads of many of the torch-bearers gave their faces a look of saint-like grace, except at such times as the evening breeze made the candle-grease refractory, and one might easily have imagined himself a spectator at a celebration in Seville.

Many bands all playing different tunes in different times and keys, rows of hard-faced, fat-stomached priests trying to look religious but failing completely to do so, and five hundred small boys, who, like ours at home, formed a sort of rear guard to the solemnities, all went to make up the peculiar performance. The whole long affair started from the church, wound through the narrow streets, and finally brought up at the church again, where it was saluted by fireworks and ringing of bells.

In the balconies of the houses that almost overhung the route were smiling crowds of lookers-on, and Roman candles and Bengola lights added impressiveness to the scene, or dropped their sparks on the garments of those promenading below. As the various images of the Virgin Mary and the Descent from the Cross passed by, everyone took off his hat and appeared deeply impressed with religious feeling. After the carriers of the floats had put down for good their expensive burdens in the vestry of the church, a few liquid refreshments easily started them quarrelling as to the merits of their respective displays. One set claimed that their Descent from the Cross was more life-like than that carried by their rivals, and they almost came to blows over which of the Virgin Marys wore the finest clothes.

Yesterday was the celebration of the expulsion of the Chinese invaders from the Philippines, about a hundred years ago, and the whole city was aglow with flags and decorations. In the afternoon everybody went to the Luneta to see the bicycle races and to hear the music. A huge crowd surged around the central plaza, and the best places in the band-stand were reserved for the Spanish ladies and Government dignitaries. The races were slow, but the crowd cheered and seemed perfectly satisfied as one after another of the contestants tipped over going around the sharp corners. After the races a beautiful Spanish maiden, whose eyes were so crossed that she must have easily mixed up the winning bicycle with the tail-ender, distributed the prizes, and the police had hard work to keep the crowd from overwhelming the centre of attraction. Then everybody listened to the music, walked or drove around in carriages, and waited for the fireworks, which were set off not long after sunset. The costly display was accompanied by murmurings of "Oh!" from hundreds of throats. There was an Eiffel Tower of flame, several mixed-up crosses that twisted in and out of each other, numerous scroll-wheels, fountains, and a burst of bombs and rockets. Some of the parachute stars gracefully floated out over the Bay and descended into the water, causing startled exclamations from the natives, who are not accustomed to look on fireworks with equanimity. But as of old, everything finally ended in smoke, and the multitude melted away, thoroughly satisfied with the celebration of the anniversary of the victory over the Chinese.

As it seems about time to take a longer rest than

usual from the labor attendant on waiting for a boom in the hemp market, I hope next week to start off on one of the well-equipped provincial steamers, that makes a run of two thousand miles south, among the sugar-islands and the hemp-ports, and in the next chapter there ought to be a rather long account of what is said to be a very interesting voyage.

VIII

A Trip to the South—Contents of the "Puchero"—Romblon—Cebu, the Southern Hemp-Centre—Places Touched At—A Rich Indian at Camiguin—Tall Trees—Primitive Hemp-Cleaners—A New Volcano—Mindanao Island—Moro Trophies—Iligan—Iloilo—Back Again at Manila.

December 23, 1894.

I HAVE just returned from the south, and feel able enough to begin the narrative. On Saturday, December 1, thick clouds obscured the sky, and gusty showers of rain continued to fall until evening, when they formed themselves into a respectable downpour. It was objectionable weather for the dry season just commencing, but the northwest monsoon was said to be heavy outside, and the rain on our east coast evidently slid over the mountains back of Manila, instead of staying where it belonged. Such was the day of starting, while, to cap the climax, just before the advertised leaving-time of the Uranus, word came from the Jesuit observatory that a typhoon was apparently getting ready to sail directly across the course we were to take, and up went signal No. 3 on the flag-staff at the mouth of the river. Philosophers, however, must not be bothered by trifles, and although my friends predicted a miserable voyage, and told me to take all my water-proofs and sou'westers, I went aboard the steamer with a smiling countenance only, followed by three "boys" who deposited my traps in a state-room of lean proportions.

At half after seven in the evening the whistle blew, the visitors departed, and the Uranus slowly began to back down the narrow river into the black night. She is one of the largest and newest "province steamers" in the Philippines, and it took a great deal of manipulation to turn her around and get her headed toward the Bay. As large, perhaps, as one of our coasting boats that runs to the West Indies, she has a flush deck from stem to stern, and is ruled over by a very jolly, stubby, little Spanish captain who looks eminently well fed if not so well groomed.

We got out of the river at eight o'clock, saw the three warning, red, typhoon lanterns glaring at us, and started full speed ahead for Romblon, our first calling-port, eighteen hours away. Dinner was served on deck from a large table formed by closing down the huge skylights to the regular dining-saloon below, and the eaters took far more enjoyment in their Spanish bill of fare under the awnings than they would have done had the same victuals been dished up downstairs. I say "victuals," for the word seems to be the only invention for just such combinations as were set before us, and "dished up" suggests the scooped-out-of-a-kettle process far better than "served." Spanish food is rather too mixy, too garlicky, too unfathomable for me, but as one can get used to anything I accommodated myself to the *puchero* (a mixture of meat, beans, sausages, cabbage, and pork), and was soon eating fish as a fifth course instead of a second. The feast began with soup and sundries, and was continued by the *puchero* which was merely an introduction to the fish course, the roast, and all the cheese and things that followed. Every dinner was practically the same, differing slightly in details, and the deck each time played its part as dining-room. Early breakfast came at six, late breakfast came at ten, and dinner poked along at five—a combination of meal hours which was enough to give one indigestion before touching a mouthful.

During the night we all waited in vain to hear the sizzling of the typhoon that came not, and got up next morning to find the scare had been for nothing. The clouds and rain were clearing away, and the prow of the Uranus was headed directly for a region of blue sky. By breakfast-time there was hardly a cloud in the heavens, the rooster up for'ard began to crow, the mooly-cow which we were soon to eat began to moo, the islands in front drew nearer, and the scene became fairer each moment. At noon we steamed below a great mountainous island, crossed a sound between it and another group, entered a narrow channel, and at one o'clock dropped anchor in the small land-locked harbor of Romblon. Everywhere the hills fell abruptly into the water, and houses looked as if they had slid down off the steep slopes to hobnob with each other in a mass below. There was a public bath down beside a brook, where everybody came to wash, an old church, the market-place, and a prodigious long flight of steps leading up to the upper districts, where the view down back over the low *nipa* houses toward the bay was most extensive.

We stayed in this little Garden of Eden until after three o'clock, then pulled out to the steamer, and left again for the south, over a calm sea and beneath a glorious sky. Some of us slept on deck in the moonlight, but, finding it if anything too cool and breezy, were up betimes to see the island of Cebu looming on our right hand. Our early six-o'clock breakfast finished, we sat up on the bridge in easy-chairs, beneath the double awning, as the Uranus poked down along the mountainous coast toward the city of Cebu. At ten o'clock we passed through the narrow channel that leads between a small island and its big brother Cebu, and soon saw the white houses of the town lapping the harbor's edge. Two Ameri-

A Citizen from the Interior.

can ships were apparently taking in their cargoes of hemp, and beside them a small fleet of native craft and steamers smudged the little bay. Anchor was dropped again and those of us who cared to go ashore met some of our former friends from Manila on 'change and took a look over this great hemp-centre of the South.

The local excitement was limited, and, except that a Chinaman had been beheaded by some enemy the night before as he was walking home through the street, news was scarce. Numerous people, however, were gathered together outside the police-station, looking at the remains, and several sailors from the American ships, who had swum ashore during the night to get drunk, were being returned to their vessels in charge of the civil guard.

The Uranus was not to stop long, and most of the through passengers returned early to the steamer to enjoy a view tempered by rather more breeze and less smell than that which the narrow streets afforded. Cebu, from the deck, was worthy of a sonnet; the white houses and church spires were set off against the dark-green background of mountains, and as the sun got lower the place did not have the broiled-alive aspect that it bore during the middle of the day. At four the stubby little Captain came aboard, and soon we turned northeast for our next stopping-place, Ormoc. Another colored sunset, another dinner in the golden light, another moonrise, another sail up among the islands, and at eleven on the evening of Monday we entered the harbor of Ormoc. Here two or three ponies were hoisted overboard to be taken landward, a can of kerosene was loaded into the purser's boat as he went ashore with the papers, and a little chorus of shoutings concluded our midnight visit to the second stop of the day.

Tuesday morning the sun rose over the lofty mountains on the island of Leyte, and the Uranus shaped her course for Catbalogan, another of the larger hemp-ports. The steam up the bay blotched with islands was perfection, and by ten o'clock the anchor hunted round for a soft bed in the ooze, some eight hundred yards off a sandy beach, above which lay the town. Those of us who had energy enough to bolt our hearty breakfast were taken by the jolly-boat onto the mud flats, and were carried through the shallow water on oars to dry land. On the slopes of the higher mountains, behind the town, the hemp-plants (looking exactly like banana-trees), grew luxuriously, and in front of many of the houses in Catbalogan the white fibre was out drying on clothes-lines. A short taste of the hot sun easily satisfied our curiosity as to Catbalogan, and we were off to the ship again for more breakfast, just as several hungry-looking Spanish guests, including the Governor's family, came aboard from the town to partake of a meal hearty enough to last them till the arrival of the next steamer.

From Catbalogan to its sister town, Tacloban, four hours to the south, the course leads among the narrow straits between high, richly wooded islands, and the scenery was most picturesque. Here and there little white beaches gleamed along the shore, and in front of the *nipa* shanties that now and then looked out from among the trees hung rows of hemp drying in the sun. Off and on the big waves, kicked up by the forward movement of the Uranus in the land-locked waters, woke up the stillness resting on the banks, and nearly upset small *banca* loads of the white fibre which was perhaps being paddled down to some larger centre from more remote stamping-grounds. From the bridge our view was most comprehensive, and it wasn't long before the steamer actually entered the river-like strait that separates the islands of Samar and Leyte. We twisted around like a snake through the narrow channel, on each side of which were high hills and mountains, richly treed with cocoanuts and hemp-plants, and, just as the sun was getting low, hauled into Tacloban, situated inside an arm of land that protects it from the dashing surges of the Apostles' Bay beyond.

At Tacloban there was little to see. A high range of hills rose behind the town, and in the evening half-light everything looked more or less attractive. We climbed a small knoll that looked off over the Bay of St. Peter and St. Paul to the south and down over the village. The strait through which we came stretched up back among the hills like a river, and in the foreground lay the Uranus. A number of hemp store-houses lined the water-front, and as usual the ever-present Chinese were the central figures of the commercial part of the community. At eight the anchor came up once more, and we left Tacloban to steam religiously down the bay of St. Peter and St. Paul for Cabalian, eight hours to the south.

Cabalian is another little hemp-town, at the foot of a huge mountain; but in the starlight of the very early morning we stopped there only long enough to leave the mail and drop a pony overboard. Sunrise caught us still steering to the south, but nine o'clock tied our steamer to a little wharf in Surigao, directly in front of a large hemp-press and store-house belonging to the owners of the ship on which we were journeying. Some of the best hemp that comes to the Manila market is pressed at Surigao, and all around were stacks of loose fibre drying in the sun or being separated into different grades by native coolies. Several of us left the ship and walked to the main village, but, as before, found little to note except the intense heat of a boiling sun.

There was the customary hill behind the town, and at the risk of going entirely into solution during the effort, two of us climbed to the top for a breath of air and a panoramic view.

Dinner came along as usual at five; but I must say that the more I ate of those curiously timed meals the less I could accommodate my mental powers to the comprehension of what I was doing. Everybody knows what a difficult psychological problem it is to determine the exact numerical nature of the feeling in the second and third toes of his feet, as compared with that in the fingers of his hands. On your hands you can distinctly feel the first finger, the middle finger, and the fourth finger; but on your feet your second toe doesn't feel like your first finger nor as a second toe should naturally feel. The great toe corresponds in sensation to one's first finger, and all the other toes save the last seem to be muddled up without that differentiated sensation which the fingers have. And so with these meals aboard ship. A ten o'clock breakfast was neither breakfast nor luncheon, and it bothered me considerably to know what in the dickens I was really eating. In fact, it affected my mind to such a degree that somehow the food tasted as if it did not belong to any particular meal, but came from another order of things; and I spent long, serious moments between the courses in trying to locate the repast in my library of prehistoric sensations, just as I have often tried to locate the digit which my second toe corresponds to in feeling.

We left Surigao an hour before midnight, sailed away over moonlit seas toward the island of Camiguin, and when I stuck my head out of the port-hole at half after five next morning, the two very lofty mountain-peaks which formed this sky-scraper of the Philippines were just ridding themselves of the garb of darkness. Three of us went ashore at seven, and were introduced to a rich Indian, who, although the possessor of four hundred thousand dollars, lived in a common little *nipa* house. He invited us to see the country, fitted us out with three horses and a mounted servant, and sent us up into the mountains, where his men were working on the hemp-plantations.

We started up the sharp slopes, and were soon getting a wider and wider view back over the town and blue bay below. First the path was bounded with rice-fields, but, as we rose, the hemp plants which, as before said, look just like their relatives, the banana-trees, began to hem us in. Now and again we came to a little hut where long strings of fibre were out drying in the sun, but our boy kept going upward until we were rising at an angle of almost forty-five degrees. Everywhere the tall twenty-five-foot hemp-trees extended toward the mountain summit as far as the eye could carry, and we were much interested in seeing so much future rope in its primogenital state. Up we went across brooks, over rocks, beneath tall, tropical hardwood trees, nearly two hundred feet high, that here and there lifted themselves up toward heaven and at last came to the place where the natives were actually separating the hemp from strippings by pulling them under a knife pressed down on a block of wood. The whole little machine was so absurdly simple, with its rough carving-knife and rude levers, that it hardly seemed to correspond with the elaborate transformation that took place from the tall trees to the slender white fibre separated by the rusty blade. One man could clean only twenty-five pounds of hemp a day, and when it is remembered the whole harvest consists of about 800,000 bales, or 200,000,000 pounds per year, it seems the more remarkable that so rude an instrument should have so star a part to play. We each tried pulling the long, tough strippings under the knife that seemed glued to the block, but there was a certain knack which we did not seem to possess, and the thing stuck fast. All in all this visit to the hemp-cleaners will supply us with strong answers to letters from manufacturers who have written us to make efforts in introducing heavy machines for separating hemp from the parent tree, but who have failed to understand that a couple of levers and a carving knife are far easier to carry up a steep mountain-slope than a steam engine, and an arrangement as big as a modern reaper. We lingered about all the morning on these up-in-the-air plantations, and at noon picked our way slowly back again over the stony path to the village, glad that we didn't have to earn fifty cents a day by so laborious a method.

Leaving our host with a promise to come ashore again and use his horses in the afternoon, we went down to the long pier and rowed off to the Uranus in one of the big ship's boats that was feeding her empty forehold with instalments of hemp. In the early afternoon we again went ashore, took other ponies and started off up the coast toward a remarkable volcano, which, though not existing in 1871, has since been business-like enough to grow up out of the sandy beach, until it is now a thousand feet high. A whole town was destroyed during the growing process, but to-day the signs of activity are not so evident. The path up the mountain-side was terrifically stony and somewhat obscure. Long creepers frequently caught us by the neck, or wound themselves about our feet, in attempts to rid the ponies of their burden. It was a laborious undertaking, and it didn't look as if we should reach the crater before dark, but we kept on

How the World's Supply of Manila Hemp is Cleaned. Capacity, Twenty-five Pounds per Diem.
See page 159.

ascending, thinking each knoll would give us that longed-for look into the business office of the volcano. But in vain. It was now getting so near sunset that we feared to lose the way, and, instead of pushing on farther, we reluctantly turned about and went full speed astern. The descent was unspeakable; the horses' knees were tired; they stumbled badly; the vines and creepers snarled us up, and everyone muttered yards of cuss-words. On the way down we saw several wonderful views over the hemp-trees to the coast below, met numerous natives cleaning up their last few stalks of fibre for the day, and at last came out once more on the rough pasture-road leading to Mambajao, off which the Uranus was anchored. It was now moonlight, we all broke into a gallop for the three-quarter-hour ride to the village, and everybody, including the jaded ponies, thanked Heaven when we reached the first lights of the town.

Late the same evening the Uranus left, sailed around the island's western edge in the moonlight, and turned southward for Cagayan, on Mindanao Island, the last of the Philippines to resist subjection by the Spanish and now the scene of wars and conflicts with the bloodthirsty savages who are indigenous to the soil.

Morning introduced us to a shaky wharf and to a group of gig-drivers, who said the town was fully three miles away. We were in the enemy's country, but nevertheless two of us started off to walk to the village, following quite a party who had already taken the road. It was an hour's plod along beneath tall cocoanut-palms before we came to the main part of the settlement, surrounding the jail, court-house, and residence of the Spanish Governor. Hard by ran a river spanned by a curious suspension-bridge. It carried the high road to the village and country on the other bank, and in our party from the steamer was an engineer who had come down to inspect this structure, which but a short time ago had utterly collapsed under the strain of its own opening exercises, killing a Spaniard, and cutting open the head of the Governor's wife. Of late, however, the bridge had been repaired, and the question seemed to be, was it safe? For my benefit, as I walked over the long eight-hundred-foot span, the old bridge wobbled around like a bowl of jelly, and considering that there were alligators in the reflective waters below, I did not feel I was doing the right thing by my camera and friends to stay longer where I was. Some of the secondary cables were flimsy affairs, and inspection revealing the fact that the structure was just one-twentieth as strong as it ought to be, placards were put up to the effect that the bridge was closed except for the passing of one person at a time.

At the bridge we fell into talk with a pleasant Spaniard, who was the *interventor* or official go-between in affairs concerning Governor and natives. We asked him as to the prospects of finding some Moro arms, knives, and shields in the settlement for being in a district upon which a recent descent had been made it seemed as if the town should be rich in bloody curios. He gave us some encouragement, and off we trotted across the central plaza with its old church, on an expedition of search. It seems that all the houses around this plaza were armed to the teeth, and in time of need the whole place could be transformed into a fort. Every house in the *pueblo* had one of the newest type of Mauser rifles standing up in the corner, and in fifteen minutes fifteen hundred men could be mustered ready armed to fight the savage Moros. We really felt as if we were in one of the Indian outposts of early American days, and were quite interested in the conversation of our guide, who seemed to take a great liking to two foreigners. We went into several little huts where knives and spears were hung upon the doors, and succeeded in exchanging many of our dollars for rude, weird weapons with waving edges or poisoned points. We passed several "tamed" Moros in the street and took off some bead necklaces, turbans, and bracelets which they had on.

Further search revealed shields and hats, and before the morning turned to afternoon we had visited nearly half the houses in the village. Sometimes a tune on the ever-present piano, coaxed out by yours truly, would bring a shield from off the wall, and at others the more telling music coming from the jingling dollars was more effectual.

For dinner we went to the house of the *interventor* to lunch on some grass mixed with macaroni, canned fish, bread and water, and if I hadn't been so much occupied with our Spanish conversation I might have felt hungry. After the meal our host wanted me to take a photograph of him and his wife dressed up in a discarded theatrical costume, and it was quite as ludicrous as anything on the trip. An upholstered throne—part of the stage-setting in their play of the week before—was rigged up in the back yard, and the señor and señora, robed as king and queen of Aragon, put on all the airs of a royal family as they stood before the camera. These good people pulled the house to pieces to show us wigs, crowns, and wooden swords, and it seemed as if we should never get away. Later, however, our good friend borrowed a horse in one place, a carriage in another, helped us to go around and collect our various purchases, presented me with a shield which he took down off his own wall, and drove us back to the steamer. Here we unloaded all the stuff, and, surrounded by a curious throng of questioners, went aboard to stow our possessions away. The day had been a prolific one, and, although we had not expected to go into the curio business on the excursion, our respective staterooms were now loaded up with gimcracks that would interest the most rabid ethnographer.

Toward midnight the Uranus steamed out of the Bay of Cagayan and headed for Misamis, still farther south. Another calm night, and Saturday morning saw us approaching a little collection of *nipa* huts presided over by an old stone fort and backed up by the usual high range of mountains. Two Spanish gunboats, the Elcano and Ulloa, all flags flying, in honor of Sunday or something were at anchor in the Bay, and at eight o'clock we pulled ashore to fritter away an hour or so in looking about an uninteresting village. There was a saying here that no photographer ever lived to get fairly into the town, for the only two who had ever come before this way were drowned in getting ashore from their vessels. As I walked about the streets, several Indian women stuck their heads out of the windows of their huts seeming quite amazed to see a live picture-maker, and asked in poor Spanish how much I would charge for a dozen copies of their inimitable physiognomies.

Misamis business detained the Uranus but for a

short hour, and she then turned her head across the
Bay eastward for Iligan, the seat of all the war operations in Mindanao. During the two hours and a
half that our course led close along the hostile shore,
we had breakfast and arrived at Iligan, the most dis-
mal place in the world, about two o'clock in the
afternoon. Everything looked down-in-the-mouth
except the thermometer, and that was up in the roar-
ing hundreds. The town was like all other Philippine villages, except that around the outskirts were
the ruins of an old stockade with observation-towers,
and in the streets soldiers, both native and Spanish,
held the corners at every turn.

While I paddled across a creek to get a photograph of some friendly savages on the other bank, one
of my steamer friends went up to the Government
house to make a formal visit. It seems he found no
one at home except the wife of one of the high department officials, and she was reading the latest letters just fresh from the mail-bag of the Uranus. As I
got back from across the river I heard a tremendous
pandemonium going on in the upper story of the
building in question, and soon my fellow-passenger
came bolting down the stairs and out into the street
below. The poor woman, on reading in her freshly
opened letter that her husband, who had but recently
gone up to Manila for a week's stay, was an abscond-

er to the extent of some three hundred thousand dollars, suddenly lost her mind. He had tried to get across to China, so it seemed, but was taken on the sailing-day of the steamer, and the wife now first heard the news. So, as chairs and flower-pots came sailing out the windows or down the stairs, we wisely decided to get out of harm's way, and together walked back to the steamer-landing, musing on Spanish methods of pocket-lining.

The Moros themselves are sturdy beggars, though most picturesque ones, and the tame specimens that came into Iligan were curious in the extreme. Dressed in native-made cloths of all colors, their heads were ornamented with turbans of red and white and blue, while gaudy sashes gave them an air of aristocratic distinction which few of their northern brothers possessed. Some of them black all their teeth, others only put war-paint on their two front pairs of ivories, and while some looked as if they had no chewing machinery at all, others appeared as if they might only have played centre rush on a modern foot-ball team.

For years now Spain has sent men and gun-boats down to Mindanao to wipe out the savages and bring the island under complete subjection, but without avail. Young boys from the north have been drafted into native regiments to go south on this fatal errand. The prisons of Manila have been emptied and the convicts, armed with *bolos* or meat-choppers, have followed their more righteous brethren to the front. Well-trained native troops have gone there; Spanish troops have gone; officers have tried it, but to no end. If, in the storming of some Moro stronghold, a dozen miles back inland from the beach, the convicts in the front rank were cut to pieces by the enemy, it was of no importance. If the drafted youths were slaughtered, there were more at home. If the native troops failed to carry the charge, things began to look serious. But if the Spanish companies were touched, it was time to flee. Such have been the tactics in this great grave-yard, and where the Moros lost the day, fever stepped in and won. The towns along the coast are Spain's, but the interior still swarms with savages, who are there to dispute her advance and are daily tramping over the graves of many of her soldiers.

We left Moro land at eight o'clock in the evening, after dining various officials who came aboard to see what they could get to eat, and by Sunday morning at sunrise had crossed northward to the island of Bohol, dropping anchor in Maribojoc, a small uninteresting place with an old church, a Spanish *padre* who had not been out of town in thirty years long enough ever to see a railroad or a telephone, and the

Moro Chiefs from Mindanao. *See page 167.*

usual collection of thick-lipped natives. We stayed here to unload a lot of bulky school-desks and chairs destined to be used by the semi-naked youth of the vicinity, and a few of our company went ashore merely to walk lazily about the village.

Next, a second stop at Cebu for the mails bound Manilaward, a good-by for the second time to our friends, and the Uranus now kept back down the coast toward Dumaguete, a prosperous town on the rich sugar-island of Negros. At ten o'clock that night we were off again, and Tuesday noon ushered us in to Iloilo, the second city of the Philippines. A lot of "go-downs" (store-houses) and dwellings on the swampy peninsula made a fearfully stupid-looking place, and the glare off the sheet-iron roofs was blinding. Scarcely a foot above tide-water, Iloilo was far less prepossessing than Manila, but everyone seemed cordial, and friends were so glad to see us that we appeared to confer a favor in stopping off to see them. The surroundings of Iloilo are far more picturesque than those of Manila, and just across the bay a wooded island, whose high altitude stands out in bold contrast to the marshes over which the city steeps, gave an outlook from the town that compensated for the inlook over dusty streets and dirty quays. The English club occupied its usually central position in the commercial section of the city, and formed an oasis of refreshment in the midst of the thirsty desert of iron roofs surrounding it. And if any single stanza of verse could have been quoted to describe the feelings of a newly arrived guest, sitting in a long chair on the club piazza and looking off at the bubbling volumes of hot air rising from those roofs, it would have been that in which the poet says:

> "Where the latitude's mean and the longitude's low,
> Where the hot winds of summer perennially blow,
> Where the mercury chokes the thermometer's throat,
> And the dust is as thick as the hair on a goat,
> Where one's throat is as dry as a mummy accursed,
> Here lieth the land of perpetual thirst."

The afternoon-tea hour is perhaps more carefully observed among the English business houses here than in the capital to the north, and we left the very good little club, with its billiard-tables and stale newspapers, to join one of the regular gatherings in the large office of a friend. But tea, toast, jam, and oranges had no sooner been set before us than the deep whistle of the Uranus sounded, and those of us who were going north had to make a hurried adjournment to the neighboring wharf. Then, as everybody on deck began to say "adios," and everybody on shore "hasta la vista," the stubby little captain roared out "avante" and our steamer started for Manila, two hundred and fifty miles away.

Next morning we got our first taste of the monsoon, and it came up pretty rough as we crossed some of the broad, open spaces between the islands. There were three dozen passengers aboard ship, and everybody, including four dogs, was desperately sea-sick. But sheltering islands soon brought relief to the prevailing misery, the dogs recovered their equilibrium enough to renew the curl in their tails, and the heaving vessel grew quite still. We touched again at Romblon, on our way up, long enough to get the mail and bring off an unshaven *padre* or two, bound up to the capital for spiritual refreshment, and for the last time headed for Manila. The monsoon apparently went down with the sun; we were not troubled further with heaving waters, and early on Thursday morning passed through the narrow mouth of Manila Bay, just as the sun was rising in the east, and the full moon setting over Mariveles in the west. The Uranus made a short run across the twenty-seven miles of water to the anchorage among the shipping, and everybody bundled ashore in a noisy launch, almost before the town had had its breakfast.

In the afternoon, when the steamer came into the river, I brought all of my arms, armor, and shells ashore to the office, and the American skippers who were waiting for free breezes from the punkah began outbidding each other with offers of baked beans and doughnuts for the whole collection. At home, the house had not been blown away, but was firm as ever; the dogs rejoiced to see me back; the cat, with a crook in her tail, purred extra loudly; the ponies, that had grown fat on lazy living, pawed the stone floor in the stable; the boy put flowers on the table for dinner and peas in the soup, and the moon looked in on us in full dress. Thus ended a fortnight's trip of some two thousand miles down through the arteries of the archipelago.

IX

Club-house Chaff—Christmas Customs and Ceremonies—New Year's Calls—A Dance at the English Club—The Royal Exposition of the Philippines—Fireworks on the King's Fête Day—Electric Lights and the Natives—The Manila Observatory—A Hospitable Governor—The Convent at Antipolo.

December 26th.

"'A YOUNG Bostonian, in business in the Philippines,' that is you, isn't it?"

"'Trembling like a blushing bride before the altar.'" "Well, blushing bride, how are you?"

"'The bells in the old church rang out a wild, warning plea.' They did, did they? And did, 'The lowing herd wind slowly o'er the lea?'"

"'The fishermen's wives were sitting on their saucepans, furniture, and babies, to keep them from sailing off skyward.' Poor things! Quite witty, weren't they?"

These were some of the expressions that greeted me as I entered the Club the other evening, about two hours after the last mail arrived.

My attention was called to the bulletin-board where the official notices were posted, and there, tacked up in all its glory was a printed copy of my letter on the typhoon, while on all sides were various members of the English colony, laughing boisterously, and poking me in the ribs with canes and billiard-cues. Some of the brokers had apparently learned the contents of that fatal letter by heart, and stood on chairs reciting those touching lines in dialogue with unharnessed levity.

To say that I was mildly flummuxed at hearing my familiar verbiage proceeding from the mouths of others would be mild, but it was impossible not to join in the general laugh, and digest, in an offhand way, the jibes and jokes which were epidemic. It seems my cautions have been of no avail, and the letter which you so kindly gave the Boston editor to read and print was sent out here to my facetious friend the American broker, whose whole life seems to be spent in trying to find the laugh on the other man. Somebody else also sent him a spare copy to give to his friends, and down town at the tiffin club next noon, my late entrance to the breakfast-room was a signal for the whole colony to suspend mastication and with clattering knives and clapping hands to vent their mirth in breezy epithets. But jokes are few and far between in this far Eastern land, and somebody or other might as well be the butt of them.

Just as surely as the 24th of December comes around, all the office-boys of your friends, who have perhaps brought letters from their counting-room to yours, all the chief cooks and bottle-washers of your establishment, all of the policemen on the various beats between your house and the club, and all the bill-collectors who come in every month to wheedle you out of sundry dollars, have the cheek to ask for *pourboires*. Imagine a man coming around to collect a bill, and asking you to fee him for being good enough to bring that document to hand. But that is just what the Manila bill-collector does at Christmas-tide. Then all of the native fruit-girls, who each day climb the stairs with baskets of oranges on their heads, come in with little printed blessings and hold out their hands for fifty cents.

Once out of the office, you go home to find the ice-man, the ashman, the coachman, and the cook all looking for tips, and you are compelled to feel most religiously holy, as you remember that it is more blessed to give than to receive.

Christmas-eve, somehow, did not seem natural, though the town was very lively. Some of the shops had brought over evergreen branches from Shanghai to carry out the spirit of the occasion. The streets were crowded with shoppers, everybody was carrying parcels, and if it had been cold, we might have looked for Santa Claus.

There are but half a dozen English ladies in our

little Anglo-Saxon colony, and each of them takes a turn in giving dinners, asking as her guests, besides a few outsiders, the other five. On Christmas-eve took place one of these rather stereotyped feasts, and afterward the guests went down in carriages to the big cathedral, that cost a million dollars, inside the old walled town, to hear the midnight mass. Accompanied by a large orchestra and a good organ, the mass was more jolly than impressive. The music consisted of polkas, jigs, and minuets, and everybody walked around the great building, talking and smiling most gracefully. A few of the really devout sat in a small enclosed space in the centre of the church, but they found it hard to keep awake, and their eyes were red with weeping, not for the sins of an evil world, but from opening and shutting their jaws in a series of yawns.

Just before the hour of midnight, comparative quiet ensued with the reading of a solemn prayer or two, but just as the most reverend father who was conducting the ceremonies finished bowing behind the high gold and velvet collar to his glittering gown, thirteen bells wagged their tongues that broke up the stillness of the midnight, and everybody wished everybody else "Felices Pascuas!" (Merry Christmas!) The organ tuned up, the boy-choir sang itself red, white, and blue, the priestly assistants swung

How to Sit without Chairs, or Manila Fruit-girls in a Street-Corner Attitude. *See page* 175.

the censors until the church was heavy with fragrance, and all those who had nothing else to do yawned and wished they were in bed.

After staying a little longer, our party left, and went over to the Jesuit Church near by, where a very good orchestra seemed to be playing a Virginia reel. Here were similar ceremonies modified somewhat to suit the rather different requirements of the Order, and after staying long enough not to appear as intruding spectators, we made our exit.

And now that Christmas is all over, everybody seems to be wearing a new hat, the most appropriate present that can be given in this land of sun-strokes and fevered brows.

January 5th.

The new year has come and gone, though out this way no one believes in turning over a new leaf.

It seems to be a custom to start the year by calling on all the married ladies of the colony, who make their guests loquacious with sundry little cocktails that stand ready prepared on the front verandas. Everybody makes calls, till he forgets where anything but his head is situated, and then brings up at the club out by the river-bank more or less the worse for wear. In honor of the day, the *menu* was most attractive, but many of the party were in no condition to partake, and spent the first day of the new calendar in suffering from the effects of their morning visits.

With the new year came the dance, which we bachelor members of the club gave to the English ladies in particular and to Manila society in general, as a small return for hospitality received, and it was declared a huge success. The club-house was decorated from top to toe. Two or three hundred invitations were sent out, and the *crème de la crème* of the European population were on hand, including General Blanco, the governor of the islands.

The English club rarely gives a dance more than once in five years, and when the engraved invitations first appeared there was much talk and hobnobbing among the Spaniards to see who had and who had not been invited. All the greedy Dons who had ever met any of the clubmen expected to be asked, and considered it an insult not to receive an invitation. One high official, who had himself been invited, wrote to the committee seeking an invitation for some friends. As, of course, only a limited number could be accommodated at the club-house, the invitations were strictly limited, and a reply was sent to the Spanish gentleman in question, stating that there were no more invitations to be had.

"Do you mean to insult me and my friends?" he wrote, "by saying that there are no more invitations left for them? Do you mean to say that my friends are not gentlemen, and so you won't ask them? I must insist on an explanation, or satisfaction."

For several days before the party one might have heard young women and girls who walked up and down the Luneta talking nothing but dance, and the Spanish society seemed to be divided up into two distinct cliques, the chosen and the uninvited.

The chosen proceeded at once to starve themselves and use what superfluous dollars they could collect in buying new gowns at the large Parisian shops on the Escolta. Most of the Spanish women in Manila can well afford to be abstemious and devote the surplus thus obtained to the ornamentation of their persons, since they are so fairly stout that the fires of their appetite can be kept going some time after actual daily food-supplies have been cut off. The men, however, seem to be as slender as the women are robust, and they, poor creatures, cannot endure a long fast. Nevertheless, the cash-drawers of the Paris shops got fat as the husbands of the wives who bought new gowns there grew more slender; and just before the ball came off these merchant princes of the Philippines actually offered to contribute five hundred dollars if another dance should be given within a short time, so great had been the rush of patrons to their attractive counters.

To make a long story short, after a lot of squabbles and wranglings among those who were invited and those who were not, the night of the party came, and only those who held the coveted cards were permitted by the giants at the door to enter Paradise.

Japanese lanterns lighted the road which led from the main highway to the club, and the old rambling structure was aglow with a thousand colored cup-lights that made it look like fairyland. Within and without were dozens of palms and all sorts of tropical shrubs, and the entrance-way was one huge bower-like fernery. Around the lower entrance-room colored flags grouped themselves artistically, and below a huge mass of bunting at the farther end rose the grand staircase that led above. Upstairs, the ladies' dressing-room was most gorgeous, and the walls were hung with costly, golden-wove tapestries from Japan. The main parlor formed one of the dancing-rooms and opened into two huge adjoining bed-chambers which were thrown together in one suite. All around the walls and ceilings were garlands and long festoons and wreaths, and everywhere were bowers of plants, borrowed mirrors, and lights.

Out on the veranda, overhanging the river, were clusters of small tables, glowing under fairy lamps, and the railings were a mass of verdure.

The orchestra consisted of twenty-five natives,

dressed in white shirts whose tails were not tucked in, hidden behind a forest of plants, and as the clock struck ten they began to coax from their instruments a dreamy waltz. The guests began to pour in— Spanish dons with their corpulent wives, and strapping Englishmen with their leaner better halves. The Spaniards, sniffing the air, all looked longingly toward the supper-rooms, while the ladies who came with them ambled toward the powder and paint boxes in the boudoir. I suppose about two hundred people in all were on hand, and the sight was indeed gay. After every one had become duly hot from dancing or duly hungry from waiting, supper was served, and there was almost a panic as the Spanish element with one accord made for the large room at the extreme other end of the building, where dozens of small tables glistened below candelabra with red shades, and improvised benches groaned under the weight of a great variety of refreshments.

Soon the slender *caballeros* got to look fatter in the face, and the double chins of their ladies grew doubler every moment. Knives, forks, and spoons were all going at once, and talk was suspended. But the room presented a pretty sight, with its fourscore couples sitting around beneath the swaying punkahs, and the soft warm light made beauties out of many ordinary-looking persons.

After everybody was satisfied, dancing was resumed in the big front rooms on the river, and the gayety went on; but the heavy supper made many of the foreign guests grow dull, and the cool hours of early morning saw everyone depart, carrying with them or in them food enough for many days.

Thus ended the great ball given to balance the debt of hospitality owed by the bachelors to their married friends, and now will come the committee's collectors for money to pay the piper.

January 31st.

Manila has been quite outdoing herself lately, and the gayeties have been numerous. The opening of the Royal Exposition of the Philippines took place last week, and was quite as elaborate as the name itself.

The Exposition buildings were grouped along the raised ground filled in on the paddy-fields, by the side of the broad avenue that divides our suburb of Malate from that of Ermita, and runs straight back inland from the sea. The architecture is good, the buildings numerous, and with grounds tastefully decorated with plants and fountains, it is, in a way, like a pocket edition of the Chicago Exposition.

Everybody in town was invited to attend the opening ceremonies by a gorgeously gotten-up invitation, and interesting catalogues of the purpose of the exhibition and its exhibits were issued in both Spanish and English. To be sure, the language in the catalogue translated from the Spanish was often ridiculous, and announcements were made of such exhibits as "Collections of living animals of laboring class," and " tabulated prices of transport terrestrial and submarine." But all of the *élite* of Manila were on hand at the ceremonies, from the Archbishop and Governor-General down to my coachman's wife, and bands played, flags waved in the fresh breeze, tongues wagged, guns fired, and whistles blew. General Blanco opened the fair with a well-worded speech on the importance of the Philippines, of the debt that the inhabitants owed to the protection of the mother-country, and of the great future predestined for the Archipelago. And just as the speaker had finished and the closing hours of the day arrived, the new electric lights were turned on for the first time. Then all Manila, hitherto illuminated by the dull and dangerous petroleum lamps, shone forth under the radiance of several hundred arc-lights and a couple of thousand incandescent ones.

The improvement is tremendous, and the streets, which have always been dim from an excess of real tropical, visible, feelable, darkness, are now respectably illuminated.

The exposition was opened on the name-day of the little King of Spain, and every house in town was requested, if not ordered, to hang out some sort of a flag or decoration. It was said that a fine of $5 would be charged to those who did not garb their shanties in colors of some sort, and all the natives were particular to obey the law. It was indeed instructive, if not pathetic, to see shawls, colored handkerchiefs, red table-cloths, carpets, and even sofa-cushions, hanging out of windows, or on poles from poverty-stricken little *nipa* huts, and any article with red or yellow in it seemed good enough to answer the purpose. We, in turn, were also officially requested to show our colors, and I hung out two bath-wraps from our front window, articles which I had picked up on the recent excursion to Mindanao, and which the wild savages there wear down to the river when they go to wash clothes or themselves. But they likewise had enough red and yellow in their composition to fill the bill, and, together with five pieces of red flannel from my photographic dark-room, our windows showed a most prepossessing appearance.

On the Sunday after the King's name-day, a costly display of fireworks took place off the water, in front of the Luneta, further to celebrate the occasion. The bombs and rockets were ignited from large floats

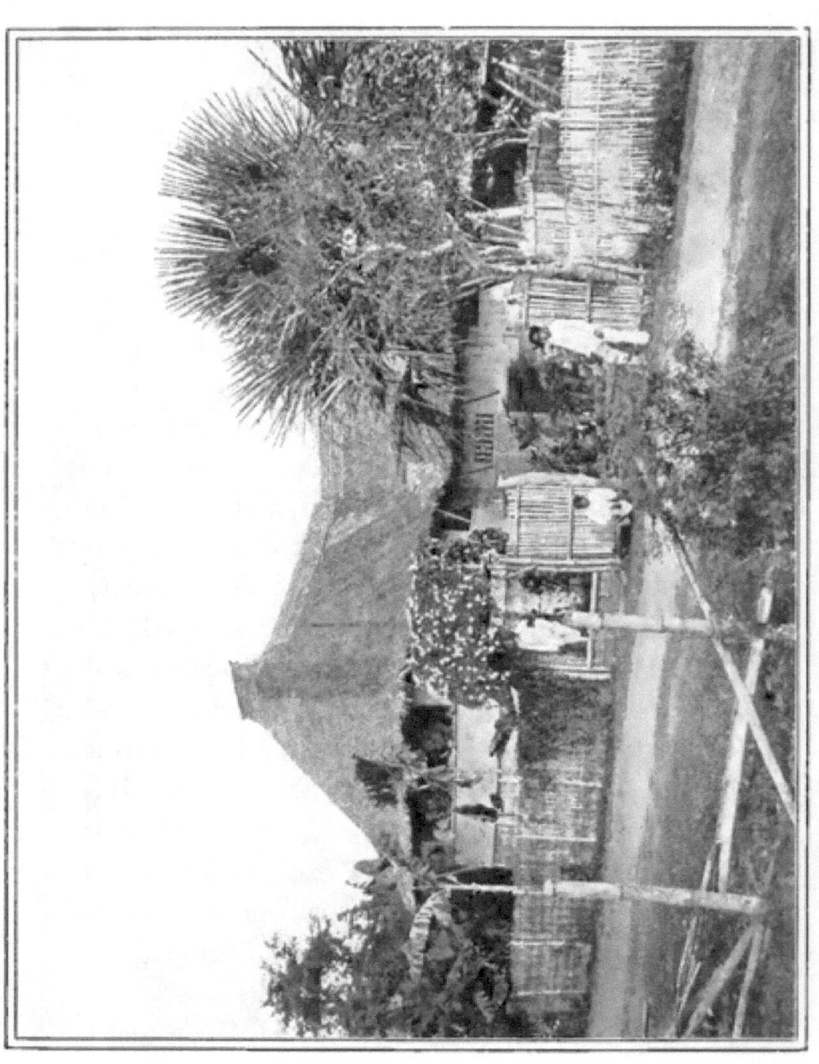

Cool, but Combustible. A Typical Nipa House. *See page 81.*

anchored near the shore, while complicated set-pieces were erected on tall bamboos standing up in the water and bolstered from behind with supports and guy-lines. The exhibition began shortly after dinner, and never had I seen a crowd of such large dimensions before in Manila. There must have been twenty-five thousand people jammed into the near vicinity of the promenade, and a great sea of faces islanded hundreds of traps of all species and genders.

The display was excellent, and both of the large military bands backed it up with good music. One of the set pieces was a royal representation of a full-rigged man-of-war carrying the Spanish flag, and she was shown in the act of utterly annihilating an iron-clad belonging to some indefinite enemy. The reflections in the water doubled the beauty of the scene, and with rockets, bombs, mines, parachutes, going up at the same time, there was little intermission to the excitement. Several rockets came down into the crowd, and one alighted on the back of a pony, causing him to start off on somewhat of a tangent. Otherwise there were no disasters, and it was nearly midnight before the great audience scattered in all directions.

The electric lights, of course, are of tremendous interest to the more ignorant natives, and every evening finds groups of the latter gathered around the posts supporting the arc-lamps, looking upward at the sputtering carbon, or examining the bugs which lose their life in attempting to make closer analyses of the artificial suns.

A fresh edition of the opera company has come out again from Italy, and performances are given Tuesdays, Thursdays, and Sundays. Everybody, as usual, is allowed behind the scenes during the intermissions, and the other evening, in the middle of a most pathetic scene in "Faust," a Yankee skipper, somewhat the jollier from a shore dinner, walked directly across the back of the stage and took his hat off to the audience. Episodes like this are hardly common, but in Manila there are not the barriers to the stage-door that exist in the U. S. A. The artillery-band on the Luneta has several times played the "Washington Post March" which you sent me, and which I gave to the fat, pleasant-faced conductor. The championship games at the tennis-court have begun, and all of the English colony generally assemble there to see the play just before sunset. Small dinners and dances are also numerous, and the cool weather seems to be incubating gayety.

February 22d.

Manila is said to have the most complete astronomical, meteorological, and seismological observatory anywhere east of the Mediterranean. Not to miss anything of such reputation, several of us decided to make a call on Padre Faure, who presides over the institution, and who is well known scientifically all over the world. At the observatory we were cordially received by an assistant, who spoke English well enough to turn us off from using Spanish, and were conducted over the establishment. Here were machines which would write down the motions of the earth in seismological disturbances, and which conveyed to the ear various subterranean noises going on below the surface. Still other instruments were so delicate that they rang electric bells when mutterings took place far underground, and thus warned the observers of approaching trouble. Another, into which you could look, showed a moving black cross on a white ground, that danced at all the slight tremblings continually going on; and the rumbling of a heavy cart over the neighboring highroad would make it tremble with excitement. A solid tower of rock twenty feet square extended up through the building from bottom to top, and was entirely disconnected with the surrounding structure. On this column all of the earthquake-instruments were arranged; and any sort of an oscillation that took place would be recorded in ink on charts arranged for the purpose. Various wires and electric connections were everywhere visible, and an approaching disturbance would be sure to set enough bells and tickers a-going to arouse one of the attendants.

The great school-building in which the observatory was placed was fully six hundred feet square, with a large court-yard in the centre containing fountains and tropical plants in profusion. After leaving the lower portions of the building, we ascended through long hallways, to visit the meteorological department above. Barometers, thermometers, wind-gauges, rain-measurers, and all sorts of recording instruments filled a most interesting room; and Padre Faure gave us a long discourse on typhoons, earthquakes, and various other phenomena. From the roof of the observatory a splendid view of the city, Bay, and adjacent country may be had, and Manila lay before us steaming in the sun. Before leaving, we saw the twenty-inch telescope, constructed in Washington under the direction of the Padre who was our guide, which is soon to be installed in a special building constructed for the purpose. He seemed much impressed by the United States, and at our departure presented us with one of the monthly observatory reports, which give the whole story of the movements of the earth, winds, heavens, tides, stars, and clouds, at every hour of the day and night, for every day during the month, and for every month during the year.

Last Monday was again the usual bank-holiday;

and on the Saturday before, the customary three of us who seem to be more energetic at seeing the country than our friends, decided to take another excursion up the river into the hill-country.

In the forenoon we gave orders to the boys to get ready the provisions, and meet us at the club-house in the early afternoon. Our plan was to take one of the light *randans* from the boat-house, row up the river for twelve or fifteen miles, take *carromatas* up into the hills to a place called Antipolo, and finally to horseback it over the mountains to Bossa Bossa, a lonely hill village, ten miles farther on.

The time came. All of our goods and chattels were piled into the boat. We took off white coats, put on our big broad-brimmed straw hats, turned up our trouserloons, and prepared for a long row up against the current. But, thanks to Providence, we were able to hitch onto one of the stone-lighters that regularly bring rock down from the lake district, for use on the new breakwater and port-works at Manila, and which was being towed up for more supplies. The sun got lower and lower, and finally set, just as the moon rose over the mountains. The sail in the soft light of evening was very picturesque, and the banks were lined with the usual collection of native huts, in front of which groups of natives were either washing clothes or themselves. Large freight *cascos* or small *bancas* were either being poled up-stream by heated boatmen, or were drifting lazily down with the current, and everywhere a sort of indolent attractiveness prevailed. We continued on behind the lighter until almost at the lake itself; then cast adrift and branched off into a small side-stream that ran up toward the hills in a northerly direction.

On we wound, now between a deep fringe of bamboo-trees, now between open meadows, now between groups of thatched huts, and again through clumps of fish-weirs, coming at last to a town called Cainta, nearly an hour's row from the main stream. We stopped beneath an old stone bridge that carried the main turnpike to Manila from the mountains, and were greeted by all the towns-people, who were out basking in the moonlight. They had evidently never seen a boat of the *randan* type before, and expressed much curiosity at the whole equipment. Before many moments the governor of the village appeared in the background and asked us to put up at his residence. Ten willing natives seized upon our goods and chattels, others pulled the boat up on the sloping bank, and we adjourned to the small thatched house where lived our host. The Filipinos gathered around outside, the privileged ones came in, and everybody stared. The governor did everything for our amusement; called in singing-girls, with an old chap who played on the guitar, and otherwise arranged for our entertainment. At eleven he said "Shoo" and everybody left. His wife gave us pieces of straw matting to sleep on, and we stretched out upon one of those familiar floors of bamboo slats which make one feel like a pair of rails on a set of cross-ties.

Later the family all turned in on the floor in the same manner, and soon the cool night-wind was whistling up through the apertures.

Next morning, Sunday, a hot dusty ride of an hour and a half, over a fearful road, continually ascending, brought us to Antipolo, a stupid village commanding a grand view over the plains toward Manila and the Bay beyond. To find out where we could get ponies to take us over the rough foot-path to Bossa Bossa, we called at the big *convento* where live the priests who officiate at the great white church, whose tower is visible from the capital. Mass was just over, but the stone corridors reverberated with loud jestings and the click of billiard-balls above. On going upstairs, we broke in upon a group of *padres* playing billiards, drinking beer, smoking cigars, and cracking jokes *ad libitum*. They received us cordially, did not seem inclined to talk much on religious subjects, but advised us where we might find the necessary horseflesh. Not so much impressed with their spirituality as with their courtesy, we left, got three ponies and two carriers, and started out for the ride over the mountains.

The path was narrow and steep, the sun was hot, but the scenery was good. On and up we went, until the view back and down over the lower country became most extensive. Across brooks, over stones, through gullies, and over trees carried us to the last rise, and after passing through a grove of mangoes we came to the edge of the ridge. Down below, in a fair little valley that looked like a big wash-basin, lay Bossa Bossa, a small collection of houses shutting in a big church without any steeple. Squarely up behind, on the other side of the valley, rose the lofty peaks of the Cordilleras, and the scene was good enough for the most critical.

On descending to the isolated little *pueblo*, we got accommodation in the best house of the place, belonging to the native Governor, and adjourned for rest and refreshments. All we had left to eat in our baskets were two cold chickens, three biscuits, and four bottles of soda. We sent out for more food, and in half an hour a boy came back with the only articles that the market afforded—two cocoanuts. The house in which we were seemed to be the only one in town that possessed a chair, and, as it was, we found it more comfortable to sit on the floor. This was the centre of the great hunting-district, and all around in

A Half Caste. The Little Flower-girl at the Opera. *See page 36.*

the hills and mountains deer and wild boar were abundant. During the following night it got so cold that it was possible to see one's breath, and without coverings as we were, the whole party dreamed of arctic circles and polar bears. At daylight next morning, numb with the cold, we sat down to a breakfast consisting of carabao milk and hard bread made of pounded-rice flour, and felt pretty fairly well removed from tropics and civilization. The old church, which we could see out of the window, stood in a small plaza, and the steeple, which consisted of four tall posts covered by a small roof of thatch that protected a group of bells from the morning dew, was off by itself in a corner of the churchyard. A long clothes-line seemed to lead from the bells to a native house across the street, and we learned that the sexton was accustomed to lie in bed and ring the early morning chimes by wagging his right foot, to which the string was attached.

On the return trip we met a large party of hunters coming up from Manila for a week's deer-shooting, and by noon got back to Antipolo, where we rested in the police-station to wait for our *carromatas* that were to arrive at one o'clock.

The return to Cainta was as hot and dusty as the advance, but we were pleasantly received by our friend the governor, who had instructed the "boys" to have the refreshments ready for us. Later in the afternoon, we prepared to return to the metropolis, and the whole village came down to see us off. The governor refused to accept money for the use of his house, we were all invited to come again, and amid a chorus of cheers we shoved off for Manila.

The row down took only three hours, but on getting to the club, at moonrise, it seemed as if we had been away three weeks.

X

Exacting Harbor Regulations—The Eleanor takes French Leave—Loss of the Gravina—Something about the Native Ladies—Ways of Native Servants—A Sculptor who was a Dentist—Across the Bay to Orani—Children in Plenty—A Public Execution by the Garrote.

April 19th.

IF a ship in the Bay desires to load or discharge cargo on Sundays or religious holidays, permission can only be obtained through the Archbishop, not the Governor-General. The Easter season has come and gone, and as the Captain of the Esmeralda could not successfully play on the feelings of that highest dignitary of the church, his steamer had to lie idle for the holidays, and so miss connecting with the Peking, which ought to have taken the United States mail.

The American yacht Eleanor dropped anchor in the Bay the other afternoon, and it seemed good again to see the countenances of some of our countrymen. It appears the Spanish officials did not consent to treat her with the courtesy which a yacht or war-ship merits, and went so far as to station *carabineros* on her decks, as is customary on merchant-vessels to prevent smuggling. The Eleanor presented a fine appearance as she lay among the fleet of more prosaic craft, and her rails were decorated with Gatling guns put there for the voyage up through the southern archipelagoes where pirates reign. On the Wednesday before Holy Thursday, the owner of the Eleanor decided to start for Hong Kong, that his guests might enjoy Easter Sunday in those more civilized districts that surround the English cathedral. The yacht, like any merchantman, was obliged to get her clearance papers from the custom-house before she sailed, and to that end the Captain went ashore shortly after midday. But the chief of the harbor office had gone home for a siesta, remarking that he would not return until Monday, and that any business coming up would have to wait till then for attention.

"But I must have my papers," said the Captain, "for we leave to-night for China."

"Them you cannot have till Monday," replied the hireling in charge.

"Then I shall have to sail without them," answered the Captain, and he stormed out of the office to find our consul, whom he hoped would straighten matters out. But the efforts of the consul were of no avail. The king-pin of the harbor office refused to be interviewed, and the Captain of the yacht returned aboard with fire in his eye. After a council of war had been held, it was decided to sail, papers or no papers, and the two soldiers who were pacing up and down the deck were told the vessel was going to sea.

"But we won't let you go without your papers," said they.

"Papers or no papers, we are going to sea to-night," roared the Captain. "And if you fellows don't git aboard into that boat mighty quick, we'll be feeding you to the sharks."

The Gatling guns and show of rifles in the companion-way looked eloquent, and the two *carabineros*, murmuring that they would surely be killed for neglect of duty when they got ashore, were pushed down the gangway into a row-boat as the Eleanor got her anchor up, and steamed out of the Bay in the face of Providence and the southwest wind, almost across the bows of the Spanish flagship Reina Cristina. A tremendous diplomatic hullabaloo resulted. The consul was summoned, the guards were blown up by the discharge of verbal powder, and it almost looked as if our representative would have to send for war-ships. But the matter has finally been straightened out, and the passengers on the Eleanor have probably had their Easter Sunday at Hong Kong.

Curiously enough, for April, another typhoon has recently sailed through the gap in the mountains to the north of our capital, and gone swirling over to China, leaving in its wake a sunken steamer, which foundered with her living freight of close to three hundred souls. Out in front of the big steamship office across the way hundreds of natives are inquiring for their brothers or husbands or children. It seems the Gravina, a ship of the best part of a thousand tons, was coming down from the north, heavily loaded with rice, tobacco, and native boys, who, for not paying their tax bills, had been drafted into service for the purpose of being sent against the savages in Mindanao. She had only fifty more miles to go before reaching the entrance to Manila Bay, when the barometer fell, the wind hauled to the northwest, and the typhoon struck her. Her afterhatchway was washed overboard, and, deep in the water as she was, the seas washed over into the opening. As fast as fresh coverings were substituted they were ripped off and carried away. The engines became disabled, the water rushed into the boilerroom, putting out the fires, and the passengers, who were locked into the cabins, were panic-stricken. The steamer began to settle, and under the onslaught of a big sea, accompanied with terrific wind, suddenly heeled over and foundered with all on board, save three, the Captain standing on the bridge as she went down, crying "Viva España." Two natives and a

Spanish woman got clear of the ship before she sucked them under, and floated about on an awning-pole and a deck-table. Scarcely had the survivors got clear of one danger before a shark swooped down on the Spanish woman, and, attracted by her lighter color, bit off a limb. He paid no attention to the two natives kicking out their feet near by, and, though neither of them could swim a stroke, they managed to paddle ashore on their supports, after being in the water two nights and a day.

These two men, the only survivors of the large passenger-list of the Gravina, came into our office yesterday, and, after giving a graphic description of the catastrophe, easily got us to loosen our purse-strings. The accident is the worst that has occurred for many a day, and there is a gloom over the whole city. The newspapers came out with black borders, and many families are bereaved.

May 20th.

The more I see of these native servants, the more I appreciate that they are great fabricators and excuse-makers. Your boy, for example, every now and then wants an advance of five or ten dollars on his salary. His father has just died, he tells you, and he needs the money to pay for the saying of a mass for the repose of his soul. Then comes another boy, who says that by his sister's marrying somebody or other his aunt has become his grandmother, and he wants *cinco pesos*, to buy her a present of a fighting-cock or something else. This matter of relationship here in the Philippines is a most delicate one to keep control of, and in the matter of deaths, births, and marriages among your servants' relations it is very essential that you keep an accurate list of the family tree, so that you may check up any tendency on their part to kill off their fathers and mothers more than twice or three times during the year for the purposes of self-aggrandizement. As an example of this, my own boy actually had the cheek to ask me for the loan of a dozen dollars to arrange for the repose of the soul of one of his relatives I had once before assisted him to bury.

I seem to have gone a long way in my chronicles without speaking much of the native "ladies" in Manila, and I owe them an apology. But one of them the other day so swished her long pink calico train in front of a pony that was cantering up to the club with a *carromata* in which two of us were seated, that we were dumped out into a muddy rice-field by the wayside. So the apology should be mutual. The costumes worn by the women are far from simple and are made up of that brilliant skirt with long train that is swished around and tucked into the belt in front, the short white waist that, at times divorced from the skirt below, has huge flaring sleeves of *piña* fibre which show the arms, and the costly *piña* handkerchief which, folded on the diagonal, encircles the neck. They wear no hats, often go without stockings, and invariably walk as if they were carrying a pail of water on their heads. They generally chew betelnuts, which color the mouth an ugly red, smoke cigars, and put so much cocoanut-oil on their straight, black hair that it is not pleasant to get to leeward of them in an open tram-car. Otherwise they are generally the mothers of many children and often play well on the harp.

I made a call on the local dentist yesterday, and found him sitting on a wooden figure of St. Peter, carving some expression into the face. I thought I had got into a carpenter's shop instead of a dental establishment, and apologized for the intrusion. But the gentleman said he was the dentist, and dropped his mallet and chisel to usher me into his other operating-room. It is quite a jump from carving out features of apostles to filling teeth, but on being assured that he had received due instruction from an American dentist, I allowed him to proceed to business. The whole operation lasted about seven and one-half minutes, and by the time I had got out my dollar to pay him for the filling I swallowed soon after, he was again at work on Biblical subjects.

All in all it doesn't pay to neglect one's health in the Philippines, for the only English doctor that Manila boasts of has been here so long that the climate has shrivelled up his memory. After he has attended your serious case of fever or influenza for several days, he will suddenly stroll in some morning and give you a sinking feeling with the words:

"Oh, by the way, what is the matter with you?"

This is hardly comforting to one who considers himself a gone coon, but in justice to our friend the medico, I must say he never displays these symptoms to patients whose case is really getting desperate.

Tons and tons of water have been drunk up by the clouds of late, and have just now begun to be unceremoniously dumped down upon flat Manila, so that she has seemed likely to be washed into the sea. But rain has been badly needed. A long heat has made many the worse for wear, and the doctors have all said that unless the rain came soon, an epidemic would probably break out.

Before the showers began, we improved the spare time of another Sunday and bank-holiday by an aquatic excursion to some of the provincial towns away across to the north side of Manila Bay. Don Capitan, the purchaser of our fire-engine and the millionaire ship-owner who runs several lines of steamers and storehouses, was our host, and invited us to spend

Fat Set in the Philippines. Rapid Transit in the Suburbs of Manila.

the days as his guests aboard the trim paddle-wheel steamer that makes regular trips to the bay ports. Early on Sunday morning we started from the quay in front of the big hemp-press, and while the lower decks of the steamer were crowded with native market-women, fishermen, and Chinese, the more sightly portions of the upper promenade were reserved for us and provided with Vienna chairs. Breakfast was served in a large chart-room connected with the wheelhouse, and was a fitting accompaniment to the fresh sail out of the river through the shipping.

After discharging groups of passengers and freight into large tree-trunk boats at several little villages, we came at noon to Orani, the end of the outward run. The sister-in-law of the jet-black captain owned the largest house in the village, and put it at our disposal. Our advent had been heralded the day before, and a groaning table supported a sumptuous repast.

There were four of us besides the half-caste family of the captain's sister-in-law, and an old withered-up Spaniard who used to be governor of the village. Various cats roamed around under the table, and on top were toothpicks built up into cones, Spanish sausages, olives, flowers, and fruit with an unpronounceable name, that looked like freshly dug potatoes well covered with soil.

Beside each chair was a red clay jar, into which

each participator in the repast could from time to time transfer such articles as were apparently unswallowable, and all around stood thick-lipped serving boys, who looked as if they were only waiting to pour soup in one's lap, or garlic gravy down one's neck. The feast began with soup, and though the family could not well eat that with their knives, they could the remaining courses. After soup came the *puchero*, that mixture of beans, potatoes, cabbage, tough meat, pork, grass, garlic, and grease, and I steeled myself for the fray. Next came cooked hen with a limpid gravy accompaniment, and as the chicken had been alive up to within a few moments of going into the kettle, the question of attack was difficult. Then followed in succession cow's tongue and roast goat, fish, salad with sliced tomatoes, and dessert consisting of those fluffy affairs made of sugar and eggs which taste like captivated sea-foam. As is always customary, cheese and fruit were served together, but while a servant had to carry the fruit, the cheese seemed inclined to walk around by itself.

In due season all the débris was removed. A boy went in pursuit of the cheese and the table was cleared for strong coffee that looked dangerous. The mortality, however, among the party was not great, and all those who were able to get up from the table went to take a siesta.

At about four, we were awakened by the familiar noise coming from the grinding of an ice-cream freezer, and afternoon tea, consisting of chocolate, sandwiches, cakes and frozen pudding, was served half an hour later. At five we were to take a drive along the shore in the only two landaus that the place possessed, and since the *padre* who lived close by in the big church had been good enough to lend us one, we called on him in state, taking with us, for his refreshment, a small caldron of ice-cream. His greeting was right cordial, and after amusing us with stories of his many adventures, told in fluent English, he dismissed us with his blessing.

Two of our party got into his carriage, while other two went in that belonging to the governor of the town, and behind smart-stepping ponies we bowled off up the road that led west along the Bay.

Old Malthus would have been interested to see the number of children that exist in these provincial villages, and it really seemed as if at least one hundred and two per cent. of the population were kids. About eighteen infants could be seen leaning out of every window, in every native hut, and in the streets, byways, and hedges they were thick as locusts. Most of these children trailed little else than clouds of glory, since clothes were scarce and expensive. An undershirt was all that any of them seemed to wear, and only the dudes of the one hundred and two per cent. wore that.

Much to our amusement, the loiterers by the wayside everywhere saluted us with a "*Buenos tardes, Padre,*" and it appeared that since the holy father is the only one who drives regularly in a landau, the whole population thought of course we must be he, or some of his saintly brethren. And so we went until the gathering darkness compelled a return to the starting-point. An elaborate supper, consisting of hard-shelled crabs and other indigestibles, was followed by an impromptu dance and musicale, and the evening ended in a burst of song.

Next morning the little steamer took us and a load of fish and vegetables back to the capital.

July 6th.

Our modern journals, I know, rejoice to go into all the gruesome details of crime and its punishment, and many of their readers take as much morbid pleasure in poring over accounts of hangings, pictures of the culprit, diagrams of his cell, and last conversations with the jailer, as do the reporters in getting the information with which to make up long, padded articles paid for by the column. I am not morbidly curious myself, and trust you will not think I went to see the capital punishment of two murderers for any other than purely scientific reasons.

The two men who were executed on July 4th, just passed, were convicted of chopping a Spaniard to pieces to get the few dollars which he kept in his house, and to avenge themselves for harsh treatment. They were nothing more than native boys, one twenty and the other twenty-two, employed as servants in the family of the unfortunate victim. In short, they were sentenced to death by the garrote, and to the end of carrying out the decree a platform was erected in the open parade-ground behind the Luneta. But the people in the neighborhood objected. The women said they could not sleep from thinking over it, and could not bear to have their children see the scaffold. General Blanco was petitioned, and the place of execution was changed to a broad avenue that leads down through the back part of Manila, by the public slaughter-house. Surely the selection was appropriate.

On the fatal day, my colleague and I drove to the scene shortly after sunrise, and crowds of people had already begun to come together from the adjoining districts. Carriages of all classes rolled in from all directions. Chinamen with cues, natives with their wives, women with their infants, young girls and children, old men and maidens, were all there, dressed in their best clothes.

I knew it would be useless to stand in the crowd,

so I pushed over toward a *nipa* hut, whose windows, which were filled with natives, looked fairly out on the scaffold itself. In the name of my camera I asked admittance, which was cordially accorded, since we were "Ingleses," and on going to the upper floor we had a free view over the crowd below toward the fatal platform, with its two posts to which were attached two narrow seats. The crowd increased; they climbed into bamboo-trees, which bent to the ground; they tried to surge up on the lower framework of the house in which we were standing, and only desisted as the proprietress slashed the encroachers right and left with a bamboo-cane. The roofs of neighboring houses were black with people, the windows swarmed, and the street below heaved. Our hostess was pleasant, though fiery, and all she wanted in return for our admission was a photograph of herself. The favor was granted, and she gave us two chairs to sit in. The crowd increased, and the guards had hard work keeping back the struggling mass. Every available square inch of space was filled, and a sea of heads pulsated before us.

At last, cries of "*aqui vienen*" (here they come) arose, and the solemn procession came into view after its long journey from the central jail, over a mile away. First came the cavalry, then a group of priests, among whom marched a man wearing an apron, carrying the sacred banner of the Church, embroidered in black and gold. Next marched the prison officials, and behind them came two small, open tip-carts, drawn by ponies, in which travelled the condemned men, each supported by a couple of priests who held crucifixes before their eyes, exhorting them to confess and believe.

Following the carts, which were surrounded by a square of soldiers, walked the executioner himself, a condemned criminal, but spared from being executed by his choosing to accept the office of public executioner. Last of all came a small company of soldiers, with bayonetted guns, and the whole procession advanced to the foot of the steps leading to the platform.

The garroting instrument seems to consist of a collar of brass, whose front-piece opens on a hinge, and part of whose rear portion is susceptible to being suddenly pushed forward by the impulse of a big fourth-rate screw working through the post, something after the system of a letter-press. The criminal sentenced to death is seated on a small board attached to the upright, his neck is placed in the brass collar, the front-piece is snapped to, and when all is ready, the executioner merely gives the handle of the screw a complete turn. The small moving back-piece in the collar is by this means suddenly pushed forward against the top of the spine of the unfortunate, and death comes instantaneously from the snapping of the spinal cord.

The executioners in Manila have always been themselves criminals, and in breaking the spinal cords of their fellow-criminals, they certainly pay a price for keeping their own vertebræ intact. Like most men in their profession, however, they are well paid, and this operator got sixteen dollars besides his regular monthly salary of twenty, for each man on whom he turned the screw.

The sight of the unfortunate prisoners in the little carts, supported by the priests, was pitiable in the extreme, and their faces bore marks of unforgetable anguish. The priests ascended the platform, and the man with the embroidered banner was careful to stand far away at the side, for, according to the religious custom of the epoch, a condemned man who merely happens to touch the standard of the Church on his way to the scaffold cannot thereafter be executed, but suffers only life imprisonment.

The executioner, in a derby hat, black coat, white breeches, and no shoes, took his position behind the post at one side of the scaffold, and the first victim was carried up out of the cart and seated on the narrow bench. He was too weak to help himself or make resistance; the black cloak was thrown over his

The Fourth of July, '95. Execution by the Garrote.
"My watch stopped and the cord-pull to my camera broke just as the screw was turned on the first man to be executed." *See page 212.*

shoulders, a rope tied around his waist, the hood drawn down over his face, and the collar sprung around his neck. Then, while two priests, with uncovered heads, held their crucifixes up before him, and sprinkled holy water over the hood and long, black death-robes, the chief prison official waved his sword, the executioner gave the big screw-handle a sudden twist till his arms crossed, and without a motion of any sort, except a slight forward movement of the naked feet, the first of the condemned men had solved the great problem.

The second poor wretch all the while cowered in the little cart, but when his turn came he ascended the steps with more fortitude. After he had put on the long black gown and hood, he seated himself on the bench at the second post and the same process was repeated. But the screw-thread seemed to be rusty, and one of the native officials helped the executioner give the handle an additional turn, for which he was promptly fined $20. The doctor tarried a few moments on the scaffold, the priests read several prayers and shook holy water over the immovable black-robed figures wedded to the posts, and then, after one of the acolytes had nearly set fire to the flowing gown of the head *padre* with his long candle, everyone descended.

The remnants of the procession returned to the

prison, the troops stationed themselves in a large hollow square around the scaffold, and two dark, motionless figures locked to two posts were left in the hot sun till noon, set out against the blue background of sky and clouds.

The crowds began to disperse, the young girls chatted and joked with each other, the curious were satisfied, and the bamboo-trees were left to lift their heads at leisure.

Thus began Manila's Fourth of July, and curiously enough, my watch stopped and the cord-pull to my instantaneous camera broke just as the screw was turned on the first man to be executed.

XI

Lottery Chances and Mischances—An American Cigarette-Making Machine and its Fate—Closing up Business—How the Foreigner Feels Toward Life in Manila—Why the English and Germans Return—Restlessness among the Natives—Their Persecution—Departure and Farewell.

August 25th.

I LOST $80,000 yesterday. Perhaps I have spoken of lottery tickets, but have failed to say what an important institution in Manila the "Lotería Nacional" really is. Drawings come each month over in the Lottery Building in Old Manila, and everybody is invited to inspect the fairness with which the prize-balls drop out of one revolving cylinder like a peanut-roaster while the ticket-number balls slide out of the other. The Government runs the lottery to provide itself with revenue, and starts off by putting twenty-five per cent. of the value of the ticket-issue into its own coffers. If all the tickets are not sold, the Lotería Nacional keeps the balance for itself and promptly pockets whatever prizes those tickets draw. Lottery tickets are everywhere, in every window, and urchins of all sizes and genders moon about the streets selling little twentieths to such as haven't the ten dollars to buy a whole one. Guests at dinner play cards for lottery tickets paid for by the losers, Englishmen bet lottery tickets that the Esmeralda won't bring the mail from home, and natives dream of lucky numbers, to go searching all over town for the pieces that bear the figures of their visions.

Four months ago I got reckless enough to plank $10 on the counter of the little shop, which, at the corner of the Escolta and the Puente de España, is said to dispense the largest number of winning tickets, and became the owner of number 1700. It sounded too even, too commonplace, to be lucky, but as it was considered unlucky to change a ticket once handed you, I trudged off and locked the paper in the safe. The drawing came, and 1700 drew $100. Fortune seemed bound my way, so I made arrangements (as so many buyers of lucky tickets do) to keep 1700 every month. My name was put in the paper as holding 1700, and for three long months I remembered to send my servant to the Government office ten days before the drawing, for the ticket reserved in my name. But for three drawings it never tempted fortune. Last week I forgot lottery and everything else in our further struggle with a new piece of American machinery which was being introduced for the first time to Manila, and woke up to-day to find it the occasion of the drawing. My ticket—uncalled for—had been sold. At noon I walked by the little *tienda* whose proprietor had first given me the fatal number, to see him perched up on a step-ladder, posting up the big prizes, as fast as they came to his wife by telephone. The space opposite the first prize of $80,000 was empty. His wife handed him a paper. Into the grooves he slid a figure 1, then a 7, and then two ciphers. Ye gods—my ticket! The capital prize—not mine! $30,000 lost because I forgot—and to think that the whole sum would have been paid in hard, jingling coin, for which I should have had to send a dray or two! But I am not quite so inconsolable as my friends the two Englishmen, who kept their ticket for two years, and at last, discouraged, sold it, Christmas-eve, to a native clerk, only to wake up next day and find it had drawn $100,000. They have never been the same since. Nor have I.

And the machine that caused all the trouble—another whim of our rich friend, the owner of the fire-engine, who saw from the catalogues on our office table that American cigarette-machines could turn out 125,000 pieces a day against some 60,000, the capacity of the French mechanisms, which were in use in all the great factories in Manila. He wanted one for his friend that ran the little tobacco-mill up in

a back street, for whom he furnished the capital.
If it worked, he was in the market for two dozen
more, and vowed to knock spots out of the big
Compañía General and Fábrica Insular.

Out came our machine some weeks ago, and with
it two skilled machinists to make it work. The big
companies pricked up their ears and appeared clearly averse to seeing an American article introduced,
which should outclass the French machines for which
they had contracted.

One morning the two machinists came to our office
and handed us an anonymous note which had been
thrust under the door of their room at the Hotel
Oriente:

"Stop your work—it will be better for you."

It was perhaps not diplomatic, but we told them the
story of the two Protestant missionaries who some
years before came to Manila and attempted to preach
their doctrines in the face of Catholic disapproval.
One morning they found a piece of paper beneath
their door in the same hotel, reading:

"You are warned to desist your preaching."

Paying no attention to the warning, they woke up
two sunrises later on to find another note beneath
the door:

"Stop your work and leave the city, or take the
consequences."

Still they heeded not; and a third paper under the door, some days later, read:

"For the last time you are warned to leave. Heed this and beware of neglect to do so."

But, like Christian soldiers, they were only the more zealous in their work.

In two days more they were found dead in their rooms—poisoned.

Our friends, the engineers, were not soothed by a relation of these facts, but kept on with their work. In three days they, too, got a second warning:

"Leave your work and go away by the first steamer."

Things began to look serious, and the more timid mechanic of the two could hardly be restrained from buying a ticket to Hong Kong.

When, however, in two more days, a third piece of yellow paper was slipped into their rooms, bearing the pencilled words, "For the last time you are told to take the next steamer," the matter assumed such proportions that we arranged to have them see the Archbishop, whose knowledge is far-reaching and whose power complete. The letters were suddenly stopped and the work on the machine carried to a successful completion.

Then came the day of trial, and invitations were extended to interested persons to view the operation.

The machine was started, and the cigarettes began to sizzle out at the rate of nearly two hundred to the minute. But scarcely had the run begun before there was a sudden jar, several of the important parts gave way, and the machine was a wreck. It had been tampered with, and it was evident that the instigators of the anonymous letters had taken this more effective means of stopping competition.

The parts could not be made in Manila; America was far away, and our two machinists have just gone home in disgust.

Is it a wonder that I forgot the lottery drawing?

Somehow there are currents of trouble in the air, and some of the old residents say they wouldn't be surprised to see the outbreak of a revolution among the natives. Peculiar night-fires have been seen now for some time, burning high up on the mountain-sides and suddenly going out. There seems to be some anti-American sentiment among the powers that be, and only last week matters came to a crisis by the Government putting an embargo on the business of one of the largest houses here, in which an American is a partner. Smuggled silk was discovered coming ashore at night, supposedly from the Esmeralda, and as that steamer was consigned to the firm in question, the authorities demanded payment of a fine of $30,000. Our friends refused, the officials closed the doors of their counting-room, our consul cabled to Japan for war-ships again, the Governor-General read the telegram, hasty summons were given to the parties concerned, heated arguments followed, and the matter was finally smoothed over on the surface.

But there seems to be a distinct feeling against us, and we have been instructed from home to prepare to leave—making arrangements to turn our business into the hands of an English firm, who will act as agents after our departure.

September 20th.

The cable has come, and we hope by next month to leave this land of intrigue and iniquity. It has treated me well, but complications are daily appearing in the business world, and if we get away without suddenly being dragged into some civil dispute it will be delightful.

I am glad to have been here these two years nearly, but it is time to thicken up one's blood again in cooler climes, and I feel these fair islands are no place for the permanent residence of an American. We seem to be like fish out of water here in the Far East, and as few in numbers. The Englishman and the German are everywhere, and why shouldn't they be? Their home-roosts are too small for them to perch upon, and they are born with the instinct to fly from their nests to some foreign land. But, America is so big that we ought not to feel called upon to swelter in the tropics amid the fevers and the ferns, and I, for one, am content to "keep off the grass" of these distant foreign colonies.

The Englishman or German comes out here on a five-years' contract, and generally runs up a debit balance the first year that keeps him busy economizing the other four. At the end of his first season, he wishes he were at home. At the end of the second, he has exhausted all the novelties of the new situation. At the close of the third, he has settled down to humdrum life. At the end of the fourth, he has become completely divorced from home habits and modern ideals. And at the close of the fifth, he goes home a true Filipino, though thinking all the while he is glad to get away. He says he is never coming back, but wiser heads know better. He has heard about America, and goes home via the States, to see Niagara and New York. But his first laundry-bill in San Francisco so scatters those depreciated silver "Mexicans," which have lost half their value in being turned into gold, that he takes the fast express to the Atlantic coast, and leaves our shores by the first steamer. At home, his friends have all got married or had appendicitis, and the bustle of London, the raw rainstorms of the cold weather and the conventionality of

Paseo de la Luneta, where the Band Played, the Breezes Blew, and Manila Aired Herself Each Afternoon. *See page 18.*

life all bring up memories of the Philippines, which now seem to lie off there in the China Sea surrounded by a halo. And so, before a year is out, he renews his contract, and at the end of a twelvemonth goes sailing back Manilaward to take up the careless life where he left it, and grow old in the Escolta or the Luneta. In London he paid his penny and took the 'bus, he lived in a dingy room, and packed his own bag. But in Manila, with no more outlay, he owns his horse and carriage, he lives in a spacious bungalow with many rooms, and he lets his servants wait on him by inches. How do I know? Oh, because we've talked it all over, now that our turn for departure comes next.

The whisperings of a restlessness among the natives continue, and it is hard to see why indeed they do not rise up against their persecutors, the tax-gatherers and the *guardia civil*. Ten per cent. of their average earnings have to go to pay their poll-taxes, and if they cannot produce the receipted bills from their very pockets on any avenue or street-corner, to the challenge of the *veterana*, they are hustled off to the *cuartel*, and you are minus your dinner or your coachman. Once in the hands of the law, they are then drafted into the native regiments for operations against those old enemies, the Moros, in the fever-stricken districts of Mindanao, and their wives or families are left to swallow Spanish *reglamientos*. They have not forgotten their brothers, who, dragged down from the north, went to the bottom in the typhoon which pushed the Gravina down. They have not forgotten the execution in the public square. They remember that the Spaniards address them with the servile pronoun "*tu*," not "*usted*," and some day they may remember not to forget. They are not quarrelsome, but they are treacherous; they are not fighters, but when they run amuck they kill right and left. They do not seem to have many wants save to be left alone, to be able to shake a cocoanut from the palm for their morning's meal, or to collect the shakings from a thousand trees and ship them to Manila; to collect the few strands of fibre to sew the *nipa* thatch to the frame of their bamboo roof, or to gather enough to fill a schooner for the capital; in fact, to be able to work or not to work, and to know that the results of their labor are to be theirs, not somebody else's.

But what has all this got to do with our hegira? These last days have been replete with the labors attendant on breaking camp before the long march. Clearings out of furniture, selling one's ponies and carriages, closing up of books, shipping of one's cases and curios on those hemp-ships that are to start on the long 20,000-mile voyage to Boston, and trying to think of the things that have been left undone, or ought to be done, have all gone to make the season a busy one.

Now that it has come down to actually leaving Manila, I begin to feel the home sickness that comes from tearing one's self away from the midst of friends and a congenial life. I shall miss the hearty Englishmen with whom I rowed or played tennis or went into the country. I shall miss the servants who got so little for making life the easier. I shall miss the ponies, the dogs with the black tongues, and the cats with the crooks in their tails; the big fire-engine which we used to run, and which has now been varnished over to save trouble in cleaning; the Luneta, with its soft breezes and good music; the walks out on to the long breakwater to see the sunset, and the hobnobbing with the old salts from the ships in the bay, who called our office the little American oasis in the midst of a great desert of foreign houses. But the clock has struck, and the Esmeralda ought early next month to start us on the forty-day voyage back to God's country.

October 22d.

Is this sleep, or not sleep? Is it reality or fancy? Am I laboring under a hallucination, a weird phantasmagoria, or are my powers of appreciation, my efferent nerve-centres and their connecting links, my sum total of receptive faculties, doing their duty? I feel hypnotized. I kick myself to see if this is real, and am only led to conclude it is by looking into my sewing-kit, where the needles are rusty, the thread gone, and the depleted stock of suspender-buttons wrongly shoved into the partition labelled "piping-cord." I never did know what piping-cord was. My socks are holy, my handkerchiefs have burst in tears, and my lingerie in general looks as if it had been used for a Chinese ensign on one of the ships that fought in the naval battle of the Yalu. For two years those garments have held together under the peculiar processes of Philippine laundering, but now that barbarians have once more got hold of them and subjected them to modern treatment, they recognize the enemy and go to pieces. And so the condition of my clothes leads me to believe I am awake, although everything else suggests the dream.

Actually away from Manila, actually eating food that is food once more, actually sleeping on springs and mattresses, putting on heavier clothes, talking the English language, meeting civilized people, and realizing what it means to be homeward bound! It seems unreal after those two years of Manila life that was so different, so divorced from the busy life of the western world; much more unreal than did the new Philippine environment appear two years ago, after jumping into it fresh from God's country, as the Captain called it.

Here we are, eight days out from Manila, steaming up through that far-famed inland sea of Japan, on the good ship Coptic, bound for San Francisco; and for the life of me those twenty-four moons just passed all seem to huddle into yesterday. Surely it was only the day before that the China was taking me and my trunks the other way. And so it takes but eight short days of new experiences, new food, new air, to efface completely the effect of seven hundred yesterdays in the Philippines. Those whole seven hundred seem now as but one, and when I think of all the housekeeping, the bookkeeping, the hemp-pressing, and the cheerful putting up with all sorts of things, they all seem to be playing leapfrog with each other in the dream of a night, and I wake up to find the pines of Japan lending a certain cordial to the air that is very grateful. We never knew what we were missing in Manila in the slight matter of eating alone until we got over to Hong Kong again, and it is perhaps just as well we didn't. To think of the "dead hen," as they call it, and rice, the daily couple of eggs, the fried potatoes, and the banana-fritters on which we have tried to fatten our frames, and then look at the bill of fare on the Coptic! We exiles from Manila have gained over five pounds in these eight days, and would almost go through another two years in the haunts of heathendom for the sake of again living through a sundry few days like the past eight, in which the inner man wakes up to see his opportunities, and makes up for lost time on soups that are not all rice and water, on fish that is not fishy, on chickens that are not boiled almost alive, on roasts that taste not of garlic, on vegetables that are something more than potatoes, on butter that is not axle-grease, and on puddings and pies that are not made of chopped blotting paper and flavored with pomatum sauces.

An exuberance of spirit must be forgiven, for so welcome is the change from the old cultivated Manila contentment that the present burst of native enthusiasm is but natural. Not that I am playing false to the Malay capital—for let it be said that when once you have forgotten the good things at home the articles which that Pearl of the Orient had to furnish went well enough indeed—but that after schooling one's taste to things of low degree it is peculiarly melodramatic to return to things of high estate.

Our send-off from Manila on the 14th was as gay as the sad occasion could warrant, and several launch-loads of the "bosses and the boys" worried out to bid us a last *adios*. The Esmeralda was to have the honor of taking us away from the place to which she had brought us, and I was thoroughly

Captain Tayler, the Genial Skipper of the Esmeralda. *See page* 227.

prepared to go through the interesting process that was needed finally to straighten me out after the peculiar twisting which the voyage from Manila to Hong Kong had given me two years before.

The sunset over the mountains at the mouth of the bay was eminently fitting in its concluding ceremonies, and it seemed to do its best for us on this last evening in the Philippines. The many ships in the fleet lay quietly swinging at their anchors. The breeze from the early northeast monsoon blew gently off the shore, and Manila never looked fairer than she did on that evening, with her white churches and towers backed up against the tall blue velvet mountains, and her whole long low-lying length lifted, as it were, into mid-air by the smooth sea-mirror between us and the shore.

Captain Tayler was as jovial and entertaining as ever, and the colony had no reason to regret being participators in the farewell. We well realized that our departure was an epoch in the life of the little Anglo-Saxon colony, and in a city where important events are registered as occurring "just after Smith arrived" or "just before Jones went away," it was essential to give the occasion weight enough to carry it down into the weeks succeeding our departure.

Our native servants came off with the bags and baggage and seemed to show as much feeling as they had ever exhibited in the receipt of a Christmas present or a box on the ear. And some of our old Chinese friends, from whom we bought bales and bales of hemp in the days gone by, came too, bringing with them presents of silk and tea. Everybody looked sad and thirsty, and made frequent pilgrimages to the saloon in quest of the usual good-by stimulant.

The Esmeralda panted to get away, and we had our last words with the motley little assemblage. We were seeing Manila and the most of them for the last time, and I confess both they and the shore often looked gurgled up in the blur that somehow formed in our eyes.

The sun sank below the horizon; the swift darkness that in the tropics hurries after it, brought the electric lights' twinkling gleam out on the Luneta and the long Malecon road running along in front of the old city, from the promenade to the river. The revolving light on the breakwater cast a red streak over the river. The white eye on Corregidor, far away, blinked as the night began, and, just as the warning of "all ashore" was sounded, the faint strains of the artillery band playing on the Luneta floated out on the breeze over the sleepy waters of the Bay.

Our friends clambered aboard the launch, the customs officers took a last taste of the refreshment that Captain Tayler gives them to make them genial, the anchor was hoisted, and, with cheers from the tug and the screeching of launch-whistles, the Esmeralda put to sea, bearing with her, in us two, half the American colony in Manila and the only American firm in the Philippines.

CONCLUSION

If one has thoughts of going out to the Philippines he should learn how to speak Spanish, and how to accept, " cum grano salis," descriptions of the country, either too glowing or too gloomy. Some have gone to Manila and liked it, others have made their retreat homeward echo with tales of weary woe about this Malay capital. To each it seems to mean something different according as he kept his health or lost it, as he fell in with the life or didn't, and as he was successful or unsuccessful in that for which he left the upper side of the globe. Before buying one's ticket for the Far East one must not be moved by the suggestions of " thoughtful " persons, who say you are going to the ends of the earth and must therefore take all sorts of clothes, pianos, and means of subsistence. Accept their sympathy but not always their advice, and if Manila be your destination, be assured you are not bound for an altogether isolated village. They may do some things out there which are not down on the programme of a day's routine in the United States. The fire-engines may be drawn by oxen, the natives—contrary to Biblical suggestion—may build the roof to their shanties first and make arrangements for underpinning afterward; women may smoke cigars, and snakes may be more effective rat-catchers than cats or terriers. But there are shops in Manila, tailors, drug-stores, parks, tramways, churches, electric lights, schools, and theatres which are not altogether unlike those in the Western world.

And, in times of peace, the capital is not an altogether bad sort of a place to live in, though I can't say as much for some of the lesser towns. One may be susceptible to fever, in which case he must avoid sleeping near the ground or going about much in the sun. He may suffer from prickly heat, in which case he will not want to take oatmeal, drink chocolate, eat mangoes, or smoke pipes. Or he may become a mark for sprue—that peculiarly oriental disease which seems to destroy the lining to one's interior—in which case the quicker he takes the steamer for Japan or for 'Frisco the better. He may run against small-pox, but ought not to take it. He will have a cold or two, but won't hear of cholera or find a native word for yellow fever. Should the wind strike in from the northwest during the wet season, he must look out for typhoons, and not be surprised if, like my friend the Englishman, he some day finds only his upright piano on the spot where his light-built house stood—the rest of his things having hastened to the next village. If he feels the ground getting restless he must look out for the oil lamps on the table, or the tiles on the roof. He must not take too cold baths, sleep in silk pajamas, or walk when he has the "peseta" to ride. And in all things he will be better off by remembering to apply that motto of the ancient Greeks, μηδὲν ἄγαν—in nothing to excess.

Manila is the new Mecca, and for some time to come she is going to be looked at on the map, talked about at the dinner-table and by the fireside, and written up from all quarters. At present this Pearl of the Orient is but a jewel in the rough, but with good men to make her laws, and her gates wide open to the pilgrims of the world, she soon should shine as brilliantly as any city in the Far East.

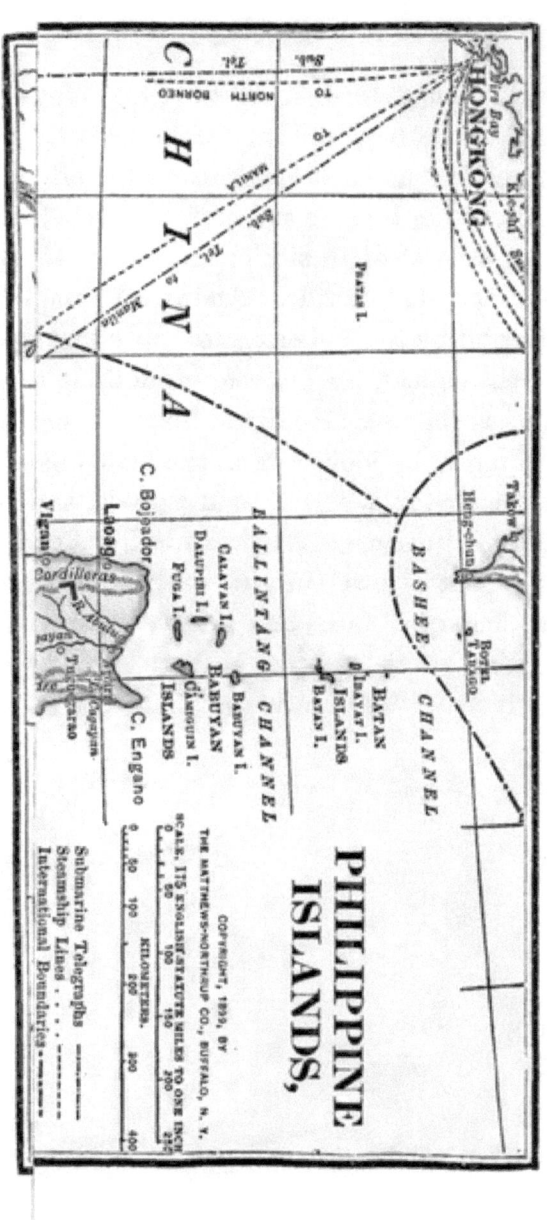

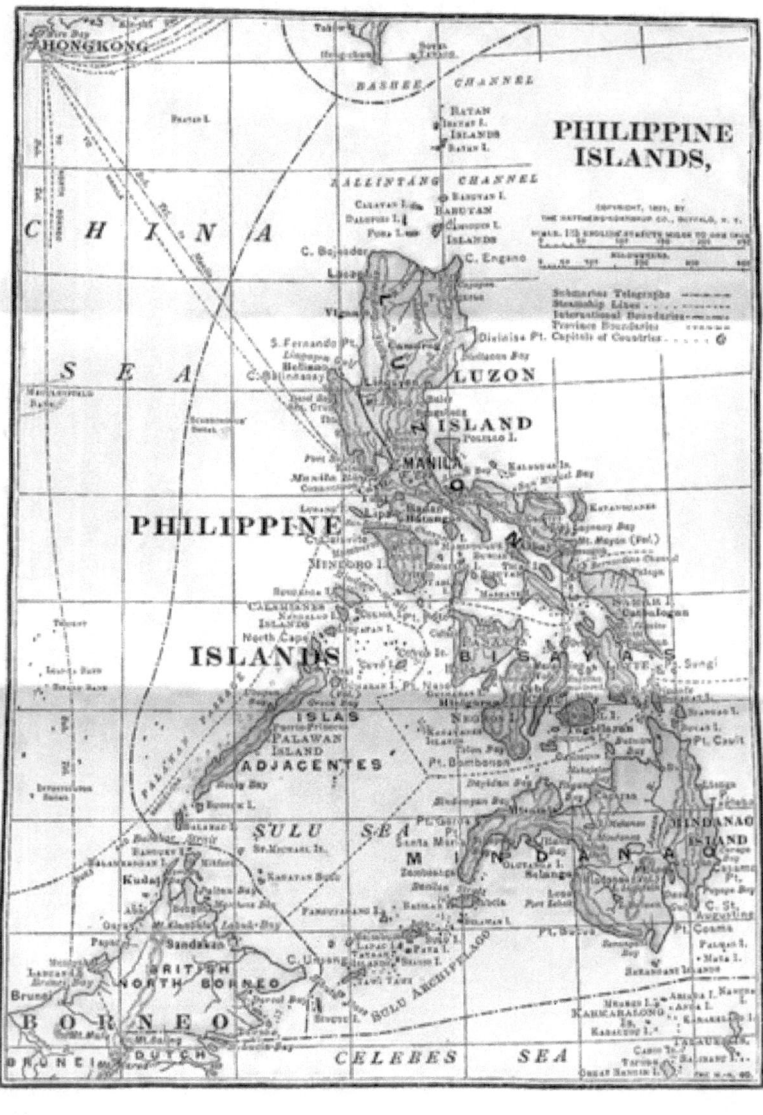

www.ingramcontent.com/pod-product-compliance
Lightning Source LLC
Chambersburg PA
CBHW030812230426
43667CB00008B/1172